Ellen

A Short Life
Long
Remembered

Chronicle Books / San Francisco

Ellen

A Short Life Long Remembered

by Rose Levit

Levit, Rose.
   Ellen; a short life long remembered.

   1. Cancer—Personal narratives. 2. Ellen.
I. Title.
   RC263.L4   362.1'9'699400924 [B]   74-4398
   ISBN 0-87701-051-X

Printed in the United States of America

Published by Chronicle Books
54 Mint Street
San Francisco, Calif. 94103   ISBN 0-87701-051-X

Contents

Acknowledgements

To protect the privacy of family members, friends, and professional people, changes were made in names as this story was written. For the same reason I have, as the author, used a pen name—one to which I feel close because of its association with my own early years.

I would like to thank the professional people, named and unnamed in this narrative, who shared in Ellen's last two years. Though words of gratitude are feeble, I thank them—for their contribution to the quality of Ellen's life, for their dedication to life itself, and for the compassion with which they supported Ellen on her way.

R. L.

Choose Life - only that and always, and at whatever risk. To let life leak out, to let it wear away by the mere passage of time, to withhold giving it and spreading it is to choose nothing.

Sister Helen Kelley

Prologue

This story cannot speak for the many other families who have lost beloved children. Each experience is unique, a strand of its own in life's complex fabric. This is a narrative which tells about one girl who was stricken by grave illness. It speaks of the possibility of beauty and growth in a life which was beset by pain and circumscribed by limitations.

It is Ellen's story—the story of some of her seventeen years. Inevitably, it becomes the story of the people who lived those days with her.

The letters are Ellen's in her exchanges with people she loved. They were found after her death. Her poems and other writings date from November 1970 through September 1972.

To Jana and Karen-lee

I

1970: DECEMBER
Diagnosis

I held a fall leaf
In the palm of my hand.
It wept bitterly
As it dropped to the ground.
To the ground, to the ground,
The cold frosted wind
Blew it to the ground.

Ellen and Troy
Words to a song
for flute and guitar

1

The distance was short, scarcely a mile. We were silent, Ellen and I, as I drove through the beginning darkness of December's early evening. Outside the slowly moving car mist-encircled street lights shone, barely able to dispel the gloom. In the quiet my thoughts circled and scattered, turning back to other drives, other silences, times of comfortable quiet between us.

This silence was different. For me, it held dread and fear, unanswered questions. I looked at Ellen, trying to guess her thoughts and feelings. She did not seem alarmed.

She did not seem aware of my fear and consternation. She seemed annoyed by the inconvenience of the next day's schedule.

In the unbroken silence, my own thoughts focused on our just-ended encounter with Dr. Talbot, our long-time friend and Ellen's physician from early childhood to this moment's age of just fifteen years. I relived the shock of Dr. Talbot's first sharp expression of incredulity, the hastily ordered and hurriedly taken pelvic x-rays and their undeniable evidence. There was a large hard mass on Ellen's right hip bone.

Automatically, unthinkingly, I shifted the car into second gear to climb the hill. Once richly covered by oaks, bay trees and madrones, the hill had been beautiful before deep cuts were made in it for the houses that now climbed like steps up its steep slope. This hill was hard for climbing on foot, difficult for planting and gardening, nearly impossible for bike riding. It was inconvenient and burdensome to us. But the view was beautiful, the large house was impressive, and David had liked it. Now David was gone from the house—trying to free himself from the feelings of obligation and entrapment in his marriage to me, trying to pursue another relationship which he deeply wanted. Jana, my older daughter, was gone, too—self-liberated from constraint and stifling parental supervision, pursuing her own exciting prematurely adult life, far away in Michigan.

We were here: Ellen and I. The large house echoed with emptiness, and the hill seemed no longer bearable. We still went up and down each day—I, hurriedly, abstractedly, driving to and from the school where I taught; Ellen struggling on foot down and up the steep slope in daily trips to the high school below.

Careful, habit-trained movements of parking the car,

silence broken by casual mention of our dinner still to be prepared—these heightened my feelings of unreality and disbelief. As we closed the garage door and unlocked the connecting door to the bottom of the house, I told myself that David would be calling, that the phone would be ringing when we reached the top of the stairs. Through all the fear and sense of unrealness, this thought felt solid and comforting. We walked carefully up the steps which, together with the hill, had given the first alarm that Ellen's right leg would not obey her, that she could not climb stairs or hills without pain and weakness in her knee.

Heavily now we went up the steps. The phone rang, and I ran ahead to answer. Ellen, leaning on the stair railing, pulled herself to follow, disengaging herself from the clumsy greeting of her dog who had waited at home, indignant at our absence. I caught the telephone.

"Yes, David, we just came home. Yes, come home. David, Ellen is sick."

2

In my relief that he had called, I did not really listen to his words. Had I listened, I would have known that he was intent on his own message, "Dr. Brent thinks I should come home while I'm working things out." To me, only the words "come home" had meaning. They meant he would return, he would share the coming days, surely he would love me.

Intent though he was on his own message, he caught my feeling of terrible alarm. And he answered out of his deep and abiding love for Ellen. "I'm coming right now!"

We awaited his coming. The humdrum of evening tasks

took over, asserting that life was ongoing, surely disaster had not befallen us. Ellen fed the dog and cat, speaking softly to the cat, authoritatively requiring patience and obedience from the dog. Numbly I went through the movements of preparing a meal, though I wondered who would eat it. Certainly not I.

For Ellen the moment of preparing for tomorrow had come. She would have to call her friend and fellow-musician Troy to say that she could not rehearse for the music program they had been planning. It had been a reluctant participation on her part, in which pleasure that he had wanted her to play her flute with him was mixed with shyness and lack of belief that she would do well.

She called; flippant words were exchanged and she hung up, distressed.

"He doesn't believe I have to go to the hospital. He thinks I just don't want to be in the program."

And then David came. The three of us—father, mother, and child—were together again.

Jana, our older daughter, was still far away but we three were now together. Distress, fatigue, disbelief, anger —what other feelings lay behind David's controlled expressionless face? He was, as he had been in past months, an enigma to Ellen and to me.

He telephoned the doctor from the privacy of our once-shared bedroom, emerging shaken and still not believing. Taking care that Ellen was not in hearing distance, he said, "He thinks it's a tumor. He thinks it's a sarcoma." Strange words, still not believed by either of us.

Ellen understood more than we knew. Behind the closed door of her own bedroom, she wrote to her sister. She wrote of her fear, of her estrangement from us, and of her disappointment in her friends.

Novato, California
December 16, 1970

Jan,

Might have a tumor somewhere in my gut. I'm scared—they're going to do all sorts of tests on me and I'm so scared. It's so big. It might be malignant. Was going to do a Christmas show type thing with Troy and another friend Thursday—flute—for a church. Instead going into the hospital for a biopsy.

I called Troy to tell him I wouldn't be able to do the show and I wanted him to say, "Listen, I'll come over and we can talk. I know you're scared." But he didn't. He didn't come through. He said, "Well, don't die on us." He didn't come through. I wanted him or Lurene or someone other than Mom or Dad to let me cry on their shoulder and comfort me. But they didn't, the way I wanted them to. No one did.

Ellen

3

The hospital in this small California city had a hometown atmosphere. Nurses, doctors, technicians were friends and neighbors. Word was already circulating that Ellen was gravely ill; the word cancer was still avoided. David signed a permission form, and Ellen was led away down the hall for what turned into hours of x-rays and tests.

We waited in the hall, sitting numbly, silently, without the comfort of conversation. During the long hours, a nurse, compassionate and friendly, put her arm on David's shoulder and murmured words of sympathy. He shook her off and walked away to stand looking out of the window into what had been an orchard years before, when the city had been the small town it still resembled.

Dismayed by the alienation, the distance between us, I could see now that though he would spend the days of waiting and share the fears of waiting with me, it was not at all certain that he would love me. It was only certain that he would love Ellen. My thoughts returned to the moments earlier that morning when we had talked with each other, and with Ellen, about her gradual loss of weight during the past months. All through the past summer and early fall, she had claimed to be on a diet. David, concerned about her thin and wan appearance, had urged Ellen's doctor to persuade her to eat more sensibly. But our friend Dr. Talbot had reassured David that Ellen's dieting and loss of weight were teenage fads, better ignored than fussed over. And I, preoccupied with my own anguish of that last summer, had concurred. Now, today, before we came to the hospital, Ellen had admitted that actually for months she had felt no desire to eat. Most foods, in fact, had been repugnant to her. Somehow during the past months she had elaborated her excuse for not eating into a diet, preferring this defense to an admission of feelings of illness.

As we waited, my thoughts went back to other times of waiting; other doctors, other hospitals, early operations. Ellen, at two, howling with outrage as she was wheeled off to surgery in the early morning, returning hours later, lying still and quiet with eyes bandaged—crossed eyes miraculously corrected, a surgeon proud of his work, parents grateful for his skill, and a child saved from strabismus and loss of vision. Earlier still, Ellen, at three months, hospitalized for surgical repair of the cleft lip with which she had been born. Through these crises we had been comforted by the conviction that, whatever the problem, it would be corrected. The price of hospitalization and painful surgery would be paid, and Ellen would be on her way again.

That there had been some positive outcome from those painful experiences, we never doubted. They had influenced Ellen in profound yet subtle ways. We saw this as we watched her grow from a small child into a tall, lithe girl. We saw her depth and sensitivity to other people, her ability to identify with and care about her friends.

In my mind's eye, I saw her again at play with Christine, friend of her early childhood days. Flashes of memory, painful now, of the long summer days of uncomplicated living in that other house, beloved place where the girls had grown up. Visions, fragmentary, but sharp and clear, like snapshots thrown together without sequence or logic: Ellen and Chris, long hair flying, towels pinned to the seats of their bluejeans, galloping across the green lawns between our houses. Not just playing horses; being horses. The sounds of their voices came back to me in the hushed still of the hospital.

"We need reins."

"Let's get blue ones."

And off into one of the homes to get strips of blue cloth.

"I'm the white one. You be the sorrel."

"I'll save you from the black stallion."

Then off again, arms flapping, towel-tails and manes flying, executing their fantasies with total involvement and seriousness as if their lives depended on 'doing it right.'

Cindy, our large white cat, running after them, knowing nothing of horse games, but swept along by the intensity of the action and the pull of closeness to Ellen.

Other times, Ellen alone, climbing the ash tree which grew on our front lawn, to sit pensively, silently, in the crook of a branch, surveying her world below.

With Jana, older by three years than she, there were earlier pre-school playtimes in that house of simple comfort and stable living, times before I returned to teaching, times when each day's high point was the return of David from his own professional world to our quiet dinner.

Summer days—Jana and Ellen in long, involved, fanciful horse and people adventures, lived out in the tall rye grass and weeds of the fields behind that beloved house of their childhood.

Winter days—long hard rains pounding on the roof, running in rivers down the large glass windows of the simple wood and stucco house. The girls playing their games inside: blankets and sheets brought out from places of storage, transforming bedrooms and living room into all kinds of imaginary abodes. Lives were lived, journeys were taken covering the long perilous distances from one tent-blanket dwelling to another. The distance across the house or from bedroom to bedroom became the stage of their play-life. Adventures took place and relationships were played out which transcended the limits of the rain-bound house.

In those years at that house, Jana and Ellen changed from small children into young girls—too soon grown. And I had watched it happen; ever-present, ever-available to offer help, maybe more help than was needed or wanted.

Now, years later, it seemed another world. Jana, scornful of restriction, unwilling to tolerate what she saw as middle class hypocrisy, was now in an explosion of rebellion. Ellen, agreeing though she did with Jana's views, was more moderate in dress and behavior than her sister. In this, she comforted my bewilderment and my own deep hurt over what seemed like Jana's total rejection of all of her past life with us.

Now, grown tall and graceful, Ellen had become increasingly straight and proud, more sure of herself, though often hesitant to put herself forward. The long, light-brown hair still sometimes fell over her face, a holdover perhaps from the early days when she had been sensitive about the scar on her lip. But more often now, her long hair was thrown back, and her large deep-brown eyes looked out straight and clear at her world.

Other memories crowded in, uncomfortable and uneasy thoughts, memories of the summer just past. That was a time when both Jana and Ellen had been dismayed and angered by my actions—unable to understand my behavior, and shaken in their belief in me.

With both girls, through their growing years, my actions had been set in a pattern of concern and interest. Sometimes over-concern and smothering interest, but always based on willingness to put their needs ahead of my own or their father's. It was a pattern which they did not always like and against which they sometimes protested. Sometimes, while listening to accounts of hurts, whether those of scraped knees or injured feelings, I had cried out indignantly, "But where was I?" As if my constant presence and vigilance could deflect the pain or cushion them from it. Their response would then be one of half-amused, half-exasperated, "Oh, Mother!" And glances of affectionate tolerance would pass between them. As they grew older, their glances took on an added dimension of knowing that they would have to reach beyond me to live their own lives. It was a knowledge which I had not yet learned to share. Up until the summer just past, I had continued to ignore their wish to loosen their ties to me. I had continued to plan, to supervise and protect, as if they were still young children. And then that summer the pattern had been shattered and, suddenly, I totally ignored them. Their problems, their needs, their pleasures and friendships had no longer touched me. I had run blindly, headlong, into the reality of my failing marriage. And again I had cried out, "But where was I?" Only this time the hurt had been my own.

That spring and summer had turned out to be a time of stark painful recognition between David and me that our marriage was in deep trouble. Months and years of drifting, of little communication between us, of desires unexpressed, of angers nursed and grudges harbored, had brought us to a point where reconciliation seemed impossible. We each now had our own careers and interests, coming together mainly in our efforts to provide a good home and be good parents. Increasingly, as the girls became adolescents and Jana in particular threw herself against the standards and limits which we asked of them, David and I found ourselves disagreeing about what was good. And then the very foundation of our marriage was shaken—since this seemed now to be its only foundation.

David had told me one day in late spring that he wanted to end the marriage, that he loved someone else. Instead of accepting with dignity, or even grudging strength, his decision to leave, that summer I had alternately pleaded with him to love me and exploded in anger when he said he could not.

In early July, after an agonizing confrontation between us, David left—went away it seemed for good. Swept by feelings of loss and anguish, ashamed to show Jana and Ellen how bereft I felt, I had closed myself up in the bedroom, which felt unbearably lonely, and tried to sleep. But sleep would not come, and the result was a brush with death through sleeping pills injudiciously taken—the accidental yet intentional component of not caring how many pills it took to win some respite from pain. And then a long sleep.

Jana and Ellen had found me. Broken by my protest, there was the vague feeling of people moving me. There was the sound of a siren cutting through the fog, disorientation, and a terrible feeling of panic over what David would think and say. The physical activities around me were never more than a blur, but my feeling of protest was sharp and real. Over and above all else, I remembered my protest. I was not willing to return. I had wanted to stay away. Between the last almost random pill and the beginning of sleep, there had been a wonderful relief and lightening of spirit, an almost joyous recognition that accidentally, yet somehow deliberately, I had rid myself of my grief. Experiencing a clear feeling of being quite separated from my body, I had felt relieved of pain and misery and it had been good.

As I sat waiting now, I knew in the reliving that the experience held, for me, deep learning about death and life. I had come out of it subdued and ashamed at causing such commotion, and pained by the resentment of my family. But beyond that I came out knowing that death could be a friend, that sometimes life's conditions can make death preferable, and that slipping away can be peaceful and even joyous.

It had been an act of weakness. Yet, as I sat and waited now, my own experience of closeness to death began to take on a different meaning for me. Dimly still, I began to feel that my own present life was a gift, one which carried its own choices. I could throw it away again, this time by weeping over Ellen's illness. Or I could use this gift of my own life to see Ellen through whatever lay ahead. It was a faint beginning of the strength which I would need to face the coming days and months.

And then again I felt the waves of uneasiness, of near-panic and despair, surge back. Was everything that Ellen had fought for, through all her past corrective surgery, to end now with something which could not be corrected? How could this be? The only way that these years could have meaning was for Ellen again to make it, again to be on her way. There would be a price, but she would surely make it.

But would she? What of the lump which I had felt once last August, the lump which showed up now as a shadow on the x-ray, the lump which the doctors now suspected was a cancerous growth in her hip bone? Last summer when Ellen had shown that lump, then much smaller, first to her father and then to me, David had said, "I don't know what it is. Ask your mother."

To me, Ellen had said reassuringly, "I think it's a muscle from the way I stand when I play my flute." David and I, both involved in our own angers and self-pities, had accepted this as an explanation.

I felt bitter self-blame. Yet I knew I had taken her to the doctor just months ago for her knee. I knew I had taken her to him just weeks ago for her dieting. Why didn't he x-ray her hip when her knee hurt her? Why didn't he see it then?

David still stood by the window, his back to me. I could not guess his thoughts, though his misery was clear. I wanted to share my thoughts with him, but it was not possible. We continued our long wait.

4

For Ellen, while we waited, the day became one of betrayal. She had been led off without breakfast, prepared for x-rays, her courage stiffened for blood tests and needles into her veins to get the needed fluid. She was not prepared for the prolonged concentration on her by doctors and technicians. She felt their urgency and haste; she experienced it as an onslaught on her dignity, a depersonalization of herself. Her adolescent shyness about exposure was ignored. In their now intense quest to identify the danger to her life, these professional people treated her as if she herself were this vague large shadow on the x-ray rather than the very frightened girl she now was.

After hours of tests, we were called to see her before she was wheeled into surgery for a biopsy. She wept with fear and anger. The three of us were trapped by the routinized activities of the hospital personnel. Ellen's dignity and privacy were violated by the push for diagnosis. Her submission was required, rather than cooperation sought. She was a thing, not a person. With her we felt this depersonalization as a sharp cutting hurt. It would greatly influence us through the long months ahead.

The doctors—pediatrician and orthopedic specialist —came after the biopsy to talk to David and me. They talked about bone cancer, osteogenic sarcoma, rare malignant disease, they said—almost always fatal. The time left for Ellen was perhaps six weeks, perhaps six months. Radiation therapy might give her some additional time, but she would have pain. They talked in short measured sentences, flat tones covering over their distress. During the past year we had consulted both doctors for Ellen's knee pains. We had asked about the weakness in her knees, about her trouble in climbing stairs and hills. A year ago, six months ago, six weeks ago, both doctors had seemed satisfied that she would outgrow whatever was causing the twinges of pain. No x-rays had been taken; no sinister causes had ever been suspected. If they now saw a connection between knee pain and bone disease, they did not say so.

We put aside our rage and misery. We listened and tried to understand the predictions. And then it was time to see Ellen who was coming out of the anesthesia. To see her, comfort and support her, and set directions for the three of us together to meet the days ahead.

5

During the days of recovering from the biopsy, we stayed, together and in turn, by Ellen's bed. At night David slept in a large chair pulled close to her side. At dawn he went home to wash and stretch out. Then I came to share the day with her. And soon David returned to read aloud to her, or just to hold her hand. Our closeness to her strengthened Ellen and cheered her. It seemed to us that she gave up a small part of her anger toward us, as she warmed herself in the comfort of our constant presence.

We talked of Jana, missing from our life for the past months. Ellen yearned to see her sister, and in the evening at home I telephoned Jana, now far away in Michigan with her friend Dennis.

Jana's voice on the phone was guarded. She had left with the heavy weight of my reproaches and her father's disapproval. Months ago in August she had decided that she must escape from the suffocation of our restrictions, complicated by the disintegrating marriage. Leaving Ellen, her sister and friend, had been hard. But she had left. Dennis had helped her to leave. And now I was calling. The message was simple.

"Jana come home. Ellen is very sick."

"But we've made plans here for Christmas. I can't come now."

I felt my tone of reproach growing heavy. Surely Jana felt it too.

"Jan, she has cancer. She wants to see you."

Suspicion, disbelief, unwillingness to be clutched at and regulated again, alternated in Jana's voice. "I'll come."

And so she came, sweeping into the airport waiting-room, wary of David and me, clothed in defiant far-out dress and coat, off-hand in the outward manner of her tenderness and concern for her sister.

We had come to the airport to meet her, Ellen still weak and unsteady, but wanting so much to greet Jana that she walked the long halls and ramps, disregarding her father's help and my anxiety. She walked ahead, intent on being there when Jana arrived.

Despite the careful outer casualness, the exchange between the girls completed for Ellen the circle of strength and love which would see her through the days ahead.

6

Dr. Alton became Ellen's doctor. It was he who confirmed the diagnosis. He set up with Ellen a relationship of truthfulness, trust, and careful listening. He told her that she had a bone-producing cancer and that he would do everything he could to help her feel better. She did not ask if this cancer would kill her. She was not ready to hear the answer. She was enraged by the simple presence of the mass, by the first hospitalization and the need for another—this time at a prestigious university hospital in San Francisco.

Here, distinguished consultants came to help determine the extent of the illness. More tests were taken to determine if metastasis, the dreaded spread of the cancer to other areas, had occurred. Long hours were spent in examinations. Residents came to question and probe. David, enraged by their disregard for Ellen's anguish over being treated as an object of study, told them to leave. He issued his own edict: only consultants requested by Dr. Alton could see Ellen.

Meanwhile Jana sat on the wide window ledge of the sixth-floor room, knees drawn up, chin resting on her clasped hands—silent witness to much that went on: the activities of the specialists who sought to teach medicine as well as to help her sister, the unthinking callousness of some of the residents, and her father's subsequent explosion into rage.

In her own anger Ellen refused to eat, swirling her food into furious designs, using forks and spoons as standing ornaments. Between consultations, examinations, and the futile mealtime demonstrations, she wrote.

> *San Francisco*
> *December 23, 1970*
>
> *Dennis,*
>
> *Bored as hell right now—back in the hospital. I expected to be shot full of all sorts of strange weird chemicals and bunches of blood tests taken, but instead I've been talking to shrinks all day. It's very depressing after awhile. I guess they think my mental state is falling apart and I'm all freaked out about having cancer.*
>
> *Shrinks are weird people—you know that? After you see enough of them you can start analyzing the way they are going to analyze you. There's the kind first off that want you to know that "they are your friend and you can tell them an-y-thing." They do that by taking up your hand, putting their hand on your shoulder—or some weird shit like that. They say—"Hi Ellen, I'm Miss So-and-so but you can call me Frances." That kind usually talk really slow and smile a lot.*
>
> *Then there is the kind that I always feel like I disappoint. They sit in the chair with their hands folded under their chins*

—waiting for me to blow open and start crying all over the place and tell them my deepest down fears. I just sit there and wait for them to ask me questions—I don't know what else to do 'cause by the way they look at me I feel like they have me all figured out before I even say nothing—so why waste my breath.

Oh—I didn't completely escape being picked at by doctors. I saw about five doctors over a period of two hours. Each one did about the same things—take temp, blood pressure, pulse, reflexes—you know, the usual, except I've had about ten thousand rectal examinations over the past week.

Jab—"Does that hurt?" they say, "does that hurt?" Jab—jab.

Of course it hurts—WHY the hell else would you be doing it?

I really dig the owls you made. Mine is sitting on the window sill next to a candle that I have burning—it's the first night of Channuka. Ha! What a drag. Happy Channuka.

Ellen

There was professional shaking of heads over Ellen's fury and uncooperativeness and over David's rage. Some of the doctors predicted a stormy path ahead for us. But Dr. Alton, who had called in the specialists, accepted the anger. He listened courteously to David, and continued to show Ellen that he was there to help her and that he would stay. The specialists agreed that surgery was impossible and would only be mutilating without providing any possibility of saving her life. Radiation therapy was recommended, and Ellen went home.

7

The experience at this hospital had one unexpected result; it was here that Frances came into Ellen's life. Young, vibrant, skilled, and beautiful, she personified all that Ellen could no longer grow up to be. She visited Ellen when David asked that a social worker talk with her and listen to her, to help where David and I could not.

At first both Jana and Ellen regarded Frances with suspicion. But suspicion gave way to grudging acceptance in that dreary hospital room. Perhaps as a test of the proffered understanding and friendliness, Ellen sought help from Frances one gray December day, help in trying to understand the puzzle that her father was to her.

They began, Ellen, David and Frances, by talking about the relationship between father and daughter, Ellen's fear of his disapproval, her rebellion at what she felt was the heavy paternal hand. Inevitably, because Ellen cared so much, their talk turned to the relationship between David and me, and Ellen's wish to have her father tell her that he had come back to stay with me. David's torment was apparent, but he could only say that he had come home to be with Ellen. His original purpose, to work out his own conflict, was lost in Ellen's greater need. And my need for a relationship of my own with him was entirely lost.

Ellen felt dismay and anger as she again had to deal with her disbelief that David could have left us for someone else, and, running counter to this disbelief, the clear evidence that he really wished he could do so. All summer and fall she had struggled with her own anguish over Jana's absence and the deep rifts between all of us. She had been unable to deal with David's withdrawal, with Jana's scorn, or with my unpredictable outbursts of anger and pleading. Now, with Frances, she began to experience another point of view. Frances was there: listening and accepting without scorn or pity, clarifying what had taken place without assigning blame or condemnation. From this sad hour in Ellen's room, there came the beginning of a friendship with Frances. Frances was there. She would be with Ellen from this day on, in friendship, with love and support.

Ellen was struggling with distress and bewilderment over her inability to separate herself from the problems of our marriage. She wanted to let go and say, "They are your problems, not mine. I'll live my own life as Jana is doing." But she could not. She could not yet understand her father's need to live his own life. She could not yet separate herself from his wish to be free. She was not yet able to see that his struggle with his own adult problems did not lessen his love for her or deny her worth.

To Ellen, at fifteen, these problems were unsolvable. She was powerless to influence the outcome of the conflict. Yet she felt deeply involved, torn by her love for both of us, and even in some strange way, guilty and self-questioning about her role or non-role in the whole complicated interaction.

To learn to deal with her feelings about us while dealing with her own deadly illness was an enormous task. Through long months of physical pain, hope and despair, joy and grief, she pursued this quest toward self-understanding as well as understanding and acceptance of the people she loved.

And I began my own private agony of reassessment, too, reliving my feelings and actions of the past year, wishing we could all go back in time so that I could repair and reshape my contribution to the events which had preceded our knowledge of Ellen's illness. Though self-blame was there, my struggle for understanding emerged more important. If I could not redo, then let me at least understand, so that in the coming days my actions could be a source of strength for Ellen and of pride for myself.

I acknowledged my actions and feelings: I perceived that my behavior—the clinging and inability to relinquish, my total despair at feeling unloved—was deeply rooted in my own childhood; that much of my self-sacrificing, overly-giving relationship with David and the girls had come from hope for a guarantee of being loved in return. Well, it had not worked. There was no such guarantee. Jana had left. David, torn by guilt and obligation, wanted to leave. And now Ellen was desperately ill, confronting me with the possibility of the ultimate leaving.

In this dilemma, I now faced just what I had most · feared and had tried through all the days of my life to avoid: letting go, relinquishing. I would have to give up, perhaps Ellen, perhaps David, perhaps both.

Jana was back now, but clearly it was for Ellen; she had already set her own terms and forced her own release.

I knew that I would have to deal in deadly earnest with my feeling about letting go of all three.

II

1971: WINTER
Radiation Therapy

---

*Bless the beasts
and the children.
Shelter them from
the storm —
Am I a beast or
a child?*

Jana

*I am a human
being. Do not fold,
spindle or mutilate.*

Writer unknown.
*Epigram found by David
and treasured by Ellen.*

1

*Clio, Michigan
December 30, 1970*

Ellen,
*Hi! Before Jana left, she suggested that I write to you which is
a compliment to us both, I guess, as we don't know each other and*

*the ability to communicate with strangers would be commendable.
I'm not much on letters, though, so bear with me.*

*First of all, I was christened Robert Jim Gipson, but I'm
known as Gypsy. I'm seventeen years old if that matters. I'm a
Cancer (June 28, 1953).*

*The song "Woodstock" by Crosby, Stills, and Nash just came
on the radio.*

*What are your interests? What do you look like anyway?
How old are you? Can you send a picture? Sorry but I don't have
one of myself yet, but I'll try to send one in my next letter. What
sign are you under?*

*My interests? Music, people, freedom, drama, dance, Love,
etc., etc., God . . .*

*How was your Christmas? Santa Claus came on a snowmobile
for us in Michigan this year and it's fabulous.*

*Do you believe in Black Magic? Do you have a philosophy of
life? Do you believe in God?*

*What do you look for in new friends, old friends, or people in
general?*

This has been a weird train of thought. Oh well!

Please try to write freely, anything that may come to mind.

*I'm usually a bit more interesting than this, I think, but I
tried.*

Oh well, please write back. Or whatever.

> *Yours in ?*
> *Love,*
> *Gypsy*

> *Clio, Michigan*
> *January 14, 1971*

Ellen!

*Hope you dug the stuff Momma sent over. She'd probably dig
knowing if you got it and all.*

Heard a story on the radio this morning about how an acid-head was tripping along Haight Street when he happened to discover the Christian Science Temple; he was immediately renewed and is now living a life of PEACE.

More news as I find it.

Please write!
Luv ya,
Dennis

Novato, Calif.
January 16, 1971

Gypsy,

Like I said, I'm bad at letter writing and usually take my time in answering them. Sorry.

Been a little down lately. People have been treating me like I'm not a whole person anymore just because I got this cancer thing. Like—

"Can I help you with this?"

"Don't you think you should take a rest?"

And always—always, always, the first thing people say to me (with deep concern in their eyes) is,

"How are you feeling?"

Oh Jesus Christ, Fuck-off!

What people don't seem to realize is that I'm alive now, right now, and that's all that matters. Why the hell do they think I'm always thinking about death. Death is just a part of life. But they shove it in front of my face when they treat me like an invalid. But you can't really blame them. They really don't know what's going on inside of me, how I'm reacting to it, so they don't know how to take me.

Poor confused suckers. That's their hang-up, not mine.

Supposed to be studying for my English final right now at school. But I don't feel like taking the time for it. School teaches you to memorize and give the right answers, but not how to think and understand. It just conditions you. Oh hell, it's just the same old shit that everybody's dissatisfied with.

Hey listen, I don't have a picture of me now, so I'll send one in my next letter. But I'll be out there with Jan sometime this spring.

Love,
El

Oak Park, Illinois
January 26, 1971

Dear Ellen,

Your mom called today. We're all so happy because she told us the radiation was going well. Ellen–I just have these great vibes that you're going to be O.K.–I know *you are. I have complete confidence in you.*

We have final exams this week. What a drag. I have a job! I work at a drugstore (at the cash register) on the weekends. It's really fun.

Thank everybody for the great Judy Collins album. I really love her music. Lately, all I've been listening to is Judy Collins, Sly and the Family Stone, James Taylor, and Joe Cocker. Some combination.

I'm taking Driver's Ed in School now. I like driving, but I'm really scared going down the highway or parking between two cars.

I just finished reading the Autobiography of Malcolm X. *It was a really good book.*

You're going to get something in the mail from me that I bought for you before Christmas, but never got to mail because the post office told me it was the wrong size box. So, I'm still looking for a box to put it in! You'll get it pretty soon, I hope.

Peace and Love to you and everyone and everything everywhere.

Your cousin,
Beth

Clio, Michigan
February 1, 1971

Dear Ellen,

Hi! Really I wish you could have written sooner.

About the fact that you have cancer. Yeah, I know. But you said something about people spending their lives being afraid and not being alive. It takes an experience of closeness with death for someone to really be able to know about living. "Though tomorrow I may be dead, today I am living forever."

A couple of kids from school turned me on to a drama course at one of Flint's art institutes. Flint and Clio aren't exactly world centers for culture or the arts, but it's a start. The class is really great though.

I'm getting some static from my Ma though, because the damn courses are the same night as catechism classes.

I'm also having trouble in my dance class because the busing has changed in Flint and my instructor can't make it to the studio the same time I can.

Mary said something about getting up the bread for your fare to Michigan next month. I'll try to help. I'd really like to get to meet you.

Yours in Him,
Gypsy

P.S. Give Jana my Love and tell her not to forget my coat; I miss it.

Love,
Me

Novato, California
February 4, 1971

Dear Gypsy,

Was good to get your letter. Me and Jana will be coming out to Michigan the second or third week in April.

The drama and dance courses sound really fine. A friend of mine had an idea for kind of a theater group. She wanted it to be a communal type thing with no leader. It wouldn't be a profit making organization either, everything would be all volunteer acting, no pay and no dues. If we could get this going it would be proof that an organization can exist without someone playing president or dictator. People would be really working together and being together. If we can get enough people interested in it, we're gonna try to put on Alice in Wonderland *for our first performance. I'll write you more about it if anything comes of it.*

Religion is really starting to get me down. Each religion believes their worship of God is the one that will get you into heaven. There's this one group that calls themselves THE WAY *and they are as smug as their name. Their way is the only way. I really shouldn't get so down on them. It's just that it's no longer the belief in God that brings them together. It's become a clique. It's cool to "belong" to* THE WAY.

I believe in God but in my own way. To me God is the Word that expresses a thought, the thought of everything, or more, the Spirit and Love of everything. God is Love. Love is something very giving, very allowing and very accepting, and so should God be.

I don't believe in Worship. Love is not worship. I feel worship is following in the steps of your ancestors, saying "Praise God" because your ancestors have always said it. Tradition. When there is tradition-following, you cannot go your own way.

Read a book called Siddartha *by Herman Hesse if you haven't already. Also maybe you'd like to look into a book called* Think on These Things *by J. Krishnamurti. It's a book on his philosophies on life. It's kind of neat to get a look into his head. He has a lot of good ideas.*

Ellen

2

Radiation therapy had begun. Morning after morning Ellen went down the hill to the high school. Absorption in English and History were impossible. But she clung to her ties with her friends; they were at school, so she went to school. Each afternoon she climbed the hill to meet Jana or me. Then we drove silently down the highway to yet another hospital where the radiotherapy was done.

Again we experienced depersonalization. This time Ellen faced a radiotherapist who seemed to her to hide behind his technicians and his awesome machine. His evaluations seemed cold and impersonal. His directions about ways to deal with side effects seemed disinterested. Perhaps he had to put emotional distance between himself and his patient. Perhaps he had to keep himself from caring about Ellen as a person since he knew he could not cure her illness.

But even if he had been the warmest and most compassionate of human beings, it could not have compensated for Ellen's violent dislike of the machine itself and the utter aloneness which she experienced while her body, lines drawn on it with marking pen, was exposed to measured doses of cobalt radiation.

As the cumulative dosage mounted, Ellen's anger increased. The skin of her abdomen burned. It turned a deep red brown. It itched and flaked. She experienced diarrhea, as each day the x-rays bombarded sick and healthy tissue. But the bone tumor decreased in size.

Revolted physically and emotionally by the x-ray process and by what she felt was coldness in the radiotherapist and his technician, Ellen began the process of facing alternatives and making choices. She could choose to terminate the therapy. But this would mean that the tumor again would grow rather than shrink.

She chose to continue. But she added her own dimension to the experience, confronting the professional people with her perceptions. At first they regarded her protests only as anger. I supported Ellen, somewhat apologetically at first, and then more clearly and openly. Together we asked for a more humane view; recognition of Ellen as a person, not just an object to be manipulated. Sensing that the gravity of her illness and the size of the tumor intimidated these professional people, making it painful for them to relate to her, Ellen forced them to relate by demanding information and requiring communication from them. Though my manner was more conciliatory than Ellen's, I supported her in this. And, as the weeks went by, a somewhat grudging admiration for the fifteen year-old girl began to emerge. They said of her, "She's gutsy. She's got spirit." And they told me long stories about other people who were without the "will to live," who came without spirit for the therapy the hospital could offer, and who died soon after.

They began to see Ellen as a human being rather than as a body with a tumor, a body with blue pen markings to delineate the radiation field.

Radiation was terminated in mid-February when the cumulative effect of the x-ray dosage was at a maximum level. Ellen's body could tolerate no more. The tumor remained, but it was smaller in size.

3

During weeks of daily trips for the dreaded treatment, some of my bonds with Ellen were reforged. We shared bitter silence and misery many days as we drove to the hospital. We shared hope as the tumor shrank. We supported each other in confrontation as we insisted on communication and relationship with the radiotherapy staff. Ellen began to put aside the anger which she felt toward me over the events of the past summer.

Jana attempted to share in the daily trips. Living in our home was a necessary burden for her if she was to share Ellen's experiences and offer emotional support. She offered to take turns with me in the driving, knowing that Ellen often preferred her company to mine. I knew this, too, but I also felt that I could protect Ellen more effectively than Jana in the daily encounters at the hospital. I could not share this role with Jana but, unfortunately, I also could not make my reasoning clear to her. Jana felt useless and alienated. She attempted to occupy herself with a half-hearted attempt at junior college courses. She was torn—wanting to be with Ellen, yet having little tolerance for living with us. She furiously rejected David's authority and was contemptuous of my lack of assertiveness in the family situation. It was a trap she wanted no part of.

She fantasied, sometimes alone, sometimes aloud with Ellen, a life in which the two sisters would share an apartment, somehow meeting their material needs and Ellen's health needs without help or contact from David and me.

4

Ellen's friendship with her friend Troy suffered. Earlier in December, when she had first told him of the illness, he had seemed flippant and casual. Now, knowing the reality of the illness, he was attempting to deal with it by surface cheerfulness and by reaching out to hold on to their relationship which seemed threatened by both the illness and the treatment. The unspoken messages were many and Ellen reacted with irritation, anger, and guilt over her anger. She wrote to her cousin Beth about her perceptions and feelings.

Novato, Calif.
February 6, 1971

Dear Beth,

I seem to write better in the middle of the night, maybe because I don't have people and their stupid needs around to bug me. I'm feeling pretty disgusted with people right now. I have had enough of them.

I have been thinking about love—love should be a very giving, very allowing and accepting kind of thing—real love is. I have a friend who expresses his love by being very open with his affection. That's a beautiful thing when someone does that, but the way Troy is affectionate is like I'm going to jump away and disappear, fade away. I'm a candy bar and if he doesn't eat me up quick, I'll melt in the sun.

I must really sound like a fickle bitch. But I'm human. I'm a person. I'm alive and I'm not going to fade away.

Troy is asking me to support him in some way. Support a need of his, bring reassurance. That isn't love, that's needing support. But it isn't important if it's love or not. What is important is that I shouldn't have to feel that I'm obligated or that I have to fill in this need for him.

No one should ask another to fulfil something in them that they can't fulfil for themselves. I feel very bad that he doesn't understand—it's a very hard thing to understand especially when you're involved in it. But he's playing the "righteous" game. He's going through the "it's all your fault" trip—what a drag. Oh hell—what a mess. Well I suppose I've talked your ear off long

enough, so I'll be off to bed.
   "Oh the games people play now
   Every night and every day now
   Never meaning what they say now
   Never saying what they mean."*
See you in the spring.

                    Love,
                    El

Ellen, herself, was feeling drained by the treatment, antagonized by the therapists, and revolted by the effects of the burning on her body. She was not able to clarify, either to herself or to Troy, her feeling that she could not now explore with him the tender and affectionate aspects of their friendship—because she was repelled and shamed by her own body. Nor was she able to say how much of her anger was really directed toward David and me.

During this unusually dry and sunny midwinter period, Ellen saw Frances once a week. In the beginning it was a cautious relationship on Ellen's part. She brought to Frances her confusion about David and me, her anger and fear about the cancer, her feelings about her sister and her friends. They talked of many things: life and living, loving and anger, problems and alternatives, illness and treatment, death and dying. As the weeks went by, Ellen found that Frances's belief in her strength made her strength a greater reality. She began to understand her feelings about Troy, and to separate them from the anger toward David and me. She found that Frances's ability to accept us while regretting our difficulties, made love for us, detached from our problems, a possibility for her too. Sometimes a remote possibility. She continued to struggle with this, even in the face of her own pain and fear.

*From the song "Games People Play," Joe South, Capitol Records.

III

Transfer Factor

---

*E*llen:
One ceases to recognize the significance of
mountain peaks if they are not viewed
occasionally from the deepest valleys.

from Dr. Al Lorin, *Spring, 1971*

1

Novato, Calif.
February 18, 1971

*D*ear Beth,

It's 3 o'clock in the morning right now and I've been thinking a lot—although my thoughts aren't too clear. So I thought I'd write you. Do you think that was a good thought? I think it was a good thought.

With the radiation shit stuff over, I can begin or try to begin to look at the whole experience clearly without having it engulf me. Like—get out of it, stand back, and observe. And I'm not sorry it happened. I'm glad as hell it's over. Oh God, I'm glad it's over —but I'm not sorry it happened. I've learned from it. I've learned how important life is, how fucking beautiful it is. Beautiful to be *alive, to love people and not be afraid of them and of life. I've learned that that's how most people spend their life—afraid—afraid of life as well as death. It's sad, it's really sad to waste your time being afraid of death when there is so much to live. Don't be afraid to live it.*

Life is so beautiful, there is so much to experience. I feel like a little kid gone hog-wild in a candy store—grabbing everything, cramming it down—in a toy store touching everything.

I'm alive! I'm more alive than before I even had the cancer because I know what it is to be alive.

Oh Lord, I just read over what I wrote. Don't think I'm trying to be righteous, O.K.? I'm not—it just came out that way. If I were you it would annoy me greatly. I can't stand it when people try to be profound all the time.

It must be 4 o'clock by now so I'll be leaving you, my dear. It was lovely chatting with you this hour of the morning, but really I must be off. Perhaps we could get together some time for tea.

Later

I'm going to be going to Michigan in April—spring vacation, I believe. Maybe we could get together.

Love,

El

2

While the radiation therapy was going on, David searched for new or different methods of treatment, for possible breakthroughs in research. He asked Frances—and as a result of her consultations with other members of the hospital staff, Dr. Al Lorin appeared in Ellen's life. A phone call from Dr. Alton to David started the contact. He spoke of another possible treatment, of experimental medicine in immunology, and of a young doctor who would like to talk with us.

Our hopes suddenly awakened, David and I met with the two doctors. The younger man spoke with measured enthusiasm and controlled intensity about something called "transfer factor." The doctors offered us an opportunity to try it, since, in any case, no other known medical treatments were curative for Ellen's illness. It would involve using a factor prepared from the white cells of the blood of our family members. They explained that, since it seemed more and more definite that cancer was virus-induced, we would have been exposed to the same virus, especially from our constant contact with Ellen, and would have built up immunity in our bodies. This factor, which protected us from the disease, might boost Ellen's own ability to fight her cancer.

David and I grasped at the opportunity. At least now we were being given a chance to fight the cancer. Even if we lost, as we were carefully warned would probably happen, at least we would fight.

The treatment was explained to Ellen. Blood was taken from both David and me to be analyzed. Then Ellen was hospitalized again, this time for a brief stay so that she could get a shot of transfer factor and have her reactions monitored in an overnight stay at the hospital. Jana had planned to stay overnight with her sister because of Ellen's apprehension about the hospital and the treatment. But, instead, Dr. Lorin made a festive occasion of initiating the treatment. With the injection of transfer factor accomplished, he kept Ellen and sent the rest of us home. He chose to watch Ellen's reactions by spending the afternoon and early evening with her outside of the hospital—sightseeing, book-browsing, and eating dinner at a small restaurant in San Francisco. He won a friend. That day, the two, young girl and her doctor, began a friendship, lightened by ribaldry and profanity on a verbal level. On a deeper, non-verbal level it included this doctor's deep involvement and commitment, and Ellen's trust and belief that he would do his best to help her.

As the weeks of late winter and early spring passed, a pattern was established. David, whose white blood cells were considered to be most effective, gave blood at three- or four-week intervals. Only the white cells were kept, the rest being returned to him. The white cells were used in the painstaking, laborious, time-consuming process of deriving the transfer factor. Then Ellen came to the Hematology Lab where Dr. Lorin injected the transfer factor into her arm muscle. Ellen found she could curse and swear at this doctor when he "shot her up" with the transfer factor, and he would laugh at her language, yet be concerned about the pain he had to cause with the shot. Despite the many ways he and his assistant tried to ameliorate the severe stinging of the injection, it remained a painful treatment—one which Ellen feared yet accepted because she felt it was her one hope for recovery.

Hope became a companion in our home that spring. Ellen prospered. Her appetite and weight increased, her energy and spirits rebounded. With the hated radiation behind her, she was cheerful and sometimes gay. She admired and trusted her doctors. Dr. Alton expressed pleasure over her progress, though he tempered his optimism by reminding David and me of the deadliness of Ellen's illness. Dr. Lorin spoke triumphantly of the increase in "rosette count" in Ellen's blood samples, a sign that her resistance was increasing. He carefully documented his research. We knew we were breaking ground and we dared to hope that Ellen would get well.

3

During that early spring, we thought again about living rather than dying. We reached out and held on to the moments of our existence, made bittersweet and poignant by the knowledge that this could be our last spring together. But as Ellen continued to prosper, our hopes rebounded. The feelings of transitoriness and limited life began to fade and we took deep breaths of pleasure and enjoyment.

We took many spur-of-the-moment trips to the ocean; including one unforgettable trip in mid-February. Inland, despite the wind, spring hinted broadly of its early California burgeoning. We felt the promise of life and Ellen, Jana, Dennis and I threw ourselves into the car with blankets and lunch and the Irish setter, Ralf. The wind increased as we drove and, when we reached the shore, the beach and sandy hills were hidden by a storm of flying stinging sand. The drive had been too long, our spirits were too high, to turn back or merely sit in the car. Perhaps, too, we felt intoxicated by the apparent success of the transfer factor. We were feeling invincible, masters of our fate and our environment, prepared to challenge the wind and sand.

We ventured out, carrying the blankets, knowing better than to carry the lunch. Ralf, ever-trustful of our judgment, trotted behind us. We made it through the dunes and, on reaching the beach, found ourselves caught in the swirling sand which seemed to fill the otherwise vast emptiness.

Jana and Dennis wrapped themselves in one blanket, Ellen and I in another. We staggered against the wind, laughing—the laughter caught and flung out into the emptiness, the dog's barking at the stinging sand particles merging crazily with the whistling of the wind. Jana and Dennis felt their way along the water's edge; Ellen and I, trailed by the dog, stayed near the greater safety of the beach dunes. Ignoring the difficulty of Ellen's leg, we trudged, leaning away from the wind, together holding the blanket like a billowing parachute, realizing it could not protect us from the flying sand. Yet we felt strong and undefeated in our battle with the wind. Perhaps just being there was a mark of our strength and invincibility. And we laughed and continued to laugh until we collapsed on the beach, covering our heads and bodies with the blanket, close to each other—a moment of breathless communion with the earth and with each other, a moment broken by the big red setter who, panicked by our sudden disappearance under the blanket, simply sat down on my head and barked.

4

Despite moments of close communication and experiences shared with Ellen, Jana was feeling increasingly useless in our day-to-day life and in the medical treatments. She had not shared, as she had hoped, in the radiation therapy. When the immunology treatment began, she offered her blood, but Dr. Lorin preferred David's. Ellen spent most of her days at school, and Jana found her own junior college courses a mere continuation of the class situations she had detested in high school. She had come home in

December because of my urgent demand and the half-openly stated belief that Ellen's days were numbered. She disagreed with Ellen's choice of a routine, dull, Monday-through-Friday schoolday life for these numbered days. She disapproved of the support which David and I gave to Ellen in this choice. Daily Jana argued with me.

"It isn't fair to Ellen. You should tell her that she will die soon. She acts as if she has forever." Surely, Jana thought, Ellen would choose other more dramatic, soul-satisfying activities if she knew how short her life would be.

But the transfer factor had changed everything for us. Ellen seemed to be improving. She talked with hope about getting well. At times, in talking about her plans or her feelings, she seemed to ignore the very fact of her illness. To all of us, it seemed that the transfer factor could cause the numbered days of Ellen's projected life to stretch on indefinitely. I found myself thinking: maybe she does have forever.

Though Jana had forced herself to stay with us for a short time, she could not face an indefinite drawn-out life in our house. She was in conflict for weeks. Dennis, visiting again with his brothers who lived nearby, wanted to return to Michigan where he and Jana had started a store. He urged her to return with him. The winter was over; Ellen seemed able to do well without Jana now, and spring in Michigan would be beautiful.

Jana and Dennis went to Berkeley for a weekend early in March. While there, acquaintances presented them with an unexpected opportunity: people they knew were driving to the Midwest, and they had room for two more passengers.

Jana called from Berkeley to tell us that she and Dennis were taking the ride to Michigan. As I begged her not to go, Jana's own will seemed to harden. She would go. She would not let me stop her. And so that Sunday in March, she and Dennis left California again.

5

When Jana left, Ellen was deeply hurt; she felt deserted. In a journal of occasional entries, she wrote to herself, hurling herself against some of the realities of her life, ignoring others, trying to organize her life and to put things into some kind of order and focus.

March 9, 1971

Here I am, sitting on my bed with this sheet of paper in front of me. It was blank just a few minutes ago. Now it is not. This must sound juvenile. But that does not matter. It is good to think yourself out on paper.

Mother once said I was the link in the family. She said she and Dad always knew exactly what should be done for me. I feel like someone made me this way because I held them together with it. I made them close. I am the link. Is that good? Was it a waste? No. Why? Nothing is a waste.

I look at people rushing around in circles and it is circles that they are in. They are a farce. The whole world is a farce. Jan said that life gives you enough problems. Why do you make more for yourselves?

Why do you glory in misery? Why do you glory in other people's misery? You are a farce.

March 11

People make me so sad. They are so sad I feel like crying for them. I feel very defeated. All the different parts of me are different people. One part of me is of one person, another part of me is of

another person. I can't find any part of me that is me. (I'm listening to the radio. I think they are playing one of the Supremes' songs speeded up. They sound like chipmunks.)
I feel quite fake. I say that I see through people. I see them running in circles and yet I'm doing the same thing. The same things keep me going. I am no different.
Be accepting of people. They need to play their society games. I think I need it too maybe.
I feel a lot better. I had to think this out. Maybe I didn't say much, but I had to get it out. I said a lot to me.

March 12

I don't feel there is anything I can really do except be absolutely honest with Mom and Dad and myself. Because if things are going to work out they're going to have to work out honestly. Those two things are things that I have worked out and gotten straight in my head, and I don't want to forget them.

March 19

It's been a long time since I have written something down. I think Troy's been feeling a little blown out too. Said he was coming over today after school. Right. But didn't. It was raining. Cool. But didn't call. I shouldn't feel down. I should rap to him about how I feel or just rap to him before I go off thinking thoughts that bring me down. Glorying in my misery. People playing their games. O.K. I see it. I feel that I am aware of it, so I can try to stay away from it. But don't get all freaked. Take it as it comes.
With my parents I want to be honest. I tried being "hero" and saving the family, but it can't be done.
Maybe he didn't come over because he was freaked or blown out or something or just didn't feel like seeing me. That's cool. It's O.K. But don't jump to conclusions.

Things were going good for a week. Why the hell do I start feeling afraid, or do I feel afraid?

I didn't get much worked out. No *I think I did, because instead of all my thoughts overflowing in my brain, I was able to kind of sort out what was. I kind of knew what was bothering me. My thoughts have been racing and jumping to conclusions. Troy said, "Thoughts and your emotions. You have a thought and then your emotions get into it and you really blow it."*

So what do you do? Keep your emotions from getting into things? No, just try to.

Another thing about parents. They mask their feeling. I'm sure they feel a lot but they don't say anything. It really annoys me. They are afraid of making the wrong move—of saying the wrong thing. They aren't real with each other. Is that a good basis for a new relationship. I think Mother feels, "Let the wound heal. Don't keep breaking it open. It will heal better that way." Maybe so.

I don't know what is inside Dad. What he is feeling.

She eagerly awaited Jana's letters, but had trouble answering. Jana had chosen Dennis and freedom over Ellen and parental restriction. It was too threatening to Ellen to acknowledge her anger at Jana over this. She retreated into depression. She continued to deal with her struggle over the family situation. She seemed to ignore the facts of her illness.

From Jana, came an enigmatic letter, perhaps an attempt to explain her reason for leaving.

Clio, Michigan
March 16, 1971

Dear El,

How goes it? Here, I am in good ways. I can relax and sort of get my old head together.

The only way to stop lying, is to tell the truth. Sometimes though, it's hard to tell the truth so it makes sense in someone else's reality—but then, who cares if it does or doesn't, right? Tell their truths if you want to communicate—This could (has) made me into a very lonely person. It's hard to know why I lie sometimes.

About realities, it's hard many-a-time to know what a situation (or yourself) actually is, *rather than what it* appears. *Mother found out the hard way.*

Then you get into the thing of "play the game." Do I want to play their reality game? I mean—do it their way and act (though I don't feel that way) and be a sell-out to myself and not be lonely?

I don't want to sell out my own mind.

> *All love,*
> *Me*
> *Jan*
> *(who the hell is that?)*

> *Novato, Calif.*
> *March 20, 1971*

Dear Jan,

After I talked with you, I couldn't cry anymore even though I wanted to. I want to get something out, but it won't come. Mom came in and saw I'd been crying. She started to cry.

Later

I feel like I'm waiting for something. I'm not impatient. I'm just waiting.

Lot's of people been offering me dope.—Hey, Ellen, want some beans? Let's smoke a joint. I want something real. Dope's not real. Lots of people really caring about each other. That's something that would be real to me. Not loving. Caring. People sharing something and being one. I think love is kind of an image in your mind or maybe it's something that comes after a long, long time—something that has to grow gradually. Maybe what Mom feels for Dad is love. Giving all of yourself? Giving totally? Something that is real and really there would be a thing to hold on to and bring you alive.

Dad just came in to talk with me and comfort me—saw I was feeling bad. I had just been thinking that when you have people caring about each other, they can see you're feeling down and they say, "Ellen you're feeling down. Let's talk. Let me hug you." Dad wanted to do that. But I didn't want it after all. I don't know why.

I went to the Health Food store yesterday. Got some soy bean milk and granola, and some bread with unbleached flour. Their stuff makes you feel really frisky.

Today I found out about this club at school. Kind of a combination ecology and back-packing club. Will be doing a lot of things: camping and getting into nature, and a lot of the type stuff we did during conservation summer school—Zero Population Growth. Sierra Club. Ecology Action. I think it's going to be really fine. Feeling good.

Sometimes I'm afraid to say anything to Mom. I feel very secretive and suspicious, like I can't tell Mom anything, or else it will backfire. But you've got something building up in you and you think you'll explode. I feel I have to be careful of what I say to Mom—just rapping out my feelings.

I'M ALIVE
El

She wrote, answering a letter from a friend who had recently moved to Mississippi. In her letter to Charlene, who did not yet know of the illness, Ellen dealt mainly with her feelings about our family's problems.

Novato, Calif.
March 28, 1971

Dear Charlene,

I'm really sorry I didn't write sooner. For a while I haven't been able to really communicate with anyone, I mean just sitting down and rapping. I haven't been able to get my thoughts clear. Been feeling mixed up.

It's raining like hell right now. It's beautiful.

When you have something and know it should be a special way but it isn't, that's when you realize its significance. That's when it becomes important to you and not before. Before, you take it for granted.

Our family is not surviving, but the people are. The people watching out for themselves are declaring themselves independent of each other and telling others, "I am a person. Treat me like one." They are becoming whole people again, not just the pieces and fragments of people that are the result of the picking and tearing and destroying of each other. The family cannot survive if the people are not whole.

I guess what I'm saying is that I think my parents should break up, because they have just about destroyed each other. We need to pick up the fragments of ourselves and become whole again. I haven't been outside of this—I have helped to destroy too.

Your town sounds like the shits—excuse me. People seem to be trying to take and grab all they can get from each other. Like out to hurt each other. Don't let them hurt you. They aren't worth getting hurt by. Not just those specific people—all people. If you get depressed and lonely, don't wait around for something to come and bring you alive again and inspire you. Be your own inspiration. Get out and find things that bring you alive. Don't wait around, because you end up doing just that—waiting. It happens too easily when you get sad.

I find myself telling you many things that Jan and I have talked about, things that when I had a hassle, she advised me on. I see a lot of my hassles in you. I guess people seem to be going through pretty much of the same things.

It's easy to write to you—I mean I feel comfortable—I can really get my thoughts out. Jan—sometimes I have a hard time writing to her. I feel she's expecting some great line of wisdom or insight from me. I guess it's my own fear of not having anything of worth to say to her. Being afraid of not having anything of worth to say to your own sister? Jesus. Pretty stupid of me.

Jana isn't married to Dennis or anything—just living in Michigan with him and his family. They have a store going in Flint. Kind of a flea market—that isn't making it too well. It's kind of like the people aren't ready for that kind of thing—the store. She says the people back there are very non-accepting of new things. But really that's kind of true of all people. It just becomes clearer in a place of unfamiliar surroundings. (Notice—I did not say "new.")

Things are very lonely here at home. This house is so big and the people far apart. But I am O.K. It gets me down once in awhile. But I am fine.

Keep strong and happy,

Love
El

Novato, Calif.
March 30, 1971

Jan,

I think one of the reasons I was having trouble writing to you was because I felt I didn't have anything worth saying, worth your hearing. You must be tired of hearing the same old hassles that you went through coming from me.

I felt obligated to write some great lines of insight and understanding because you understood the hassles in many places where I didn't and I wanted to be able to communicate with you on the same level. But I felt your life growing away from mine, becoming separate. I felt I couldn't express myself clear enough to get my thoughts across.

I'm not depressed and I'm not trying to hang on to you or anything. I never was. I'm just trying to get my thoughts clear to myself.

My flute playing has been going down. For awhile I felt like I had nothing to play for, but now I'm going into my own direction in music. I would very much like to play for people.

More later.

El

6

Although we both wished it otherwise, the relationship between David and me placed an intolerable burden on Ellen. She found it hard to live with us, not understanding the silences, the careful considerateness and distance between us, the complete concentration on her, and detachment from each other. She knew that she was the link between us. She resented the role, yet wished that she could truly bring us together or understand why we were separate.

So, more and more she turned to her friendship with Troy and his family. They were a close-knit family and they made room for her. Troy, just sixteen years old himself, chose—in sheer self-defense—to minimize Ellen's illness, to tell her she would conquer it if she put her mind to it.

In some ways, she regarded his attitude as a demand and a drain on her limited energy. During the radiation therapy, he had preferred to ignore the physically exhausting and painful effects of the treatment. He had wanted her to ignore the emotional effects, to assert mind over matter, to spend the precious time in enjoyment of shared experiences with him. Ellen had resented this, feeling that it asked more of her than she could give.

But now, with radiation therapy over and Jana gone, she turned back to Troy, to his family of sisters and brothers, and to his parents. She found friendship, love and understanding, openness of communication and small jokes in their home. Troy's mother, a registered nurse—out of her affection for Ellen and her own professional competence —was supportive to Ellen and unintimidated by the illness.

During that spring, the two young people spent many afternoons and evenings together. They shared a love for contemporary music, and they spent hours playing their flute and guitar in wordless experimentation and flow of melody. Occasionally, when pleased with a particular musical passage, they would stop and retrace it, and write words for it. This was a continuation and a deepening of their old relationship. It spoke of ongoing interests. It challenged the illness to stop them.

They turned outward too. Together, they explored organizations and movements: Marin Peace Coalition and Zero Population Growth. Both groups suited Ellen's present thinking. She fervently identified with the anti-war movement. She had, when younger, marched with me in early "unfashionable" Vietnam peace marches. Now it was part of her: appreciation for the preciousness of life and awareness of the terrible crime of inflicting death through war or any deliberate means. With her appreciation of living for the present and her realization that the cancer and radiotherapy would prevent her from ever having children, she extended her interest into population control. It meant for her the valuing of people presently alive, the preservation of the earth's resources, the acceptance of man's place in the rhythmic life cycle and ecologic scheme of life on this planet, and the resultant belief that new human beings should be added to this scheme only as the total life situation could absorb them, provide for them, value and protect them.

Inevitably too, her fifteen, near sixteen, year-old enthusiasm turned to Women's Liberation. Her deep feelings about what she saw as unfairness in the relationships between David and me, between Dennis and Jana, awakened her interest in programs, magazine articles, books, and organizations which were tuned into this interest. Here she went without Troy. He was not comfortable in this exploration. But Jana shared her interest in Women's Lib. Together they carried me along into new viewpoints and new interpretations of my own lifelong problems.

7

In the long drives to and from doctors and hospitals, Ellen often lay back silent and tired. I drove, seldom breaking these silences. But sometimes Ellen spoke the questions which crowded her thoughts.

"Do you think I can ever have a baby after the radiation?

"What will they do about the tumor if the treatments don't make it any smaller?

"Does this kind of cancer kill people?"

Mostly the questions she asked spoke of a desperate wish to believe she had a future in which it would really matter if she could not conceive and bear a child—a future in which, with the cancer contained, it would be a problem of what to do about the bony mass that still remained after radiation. At first, I had dreaded the questions, feeling unable to give answers which would be truthful but not devastating. But as the days and weeks went by, it slowly became apparent that sharing the questions might be enough for now, that sharing an exploration of possible answers could be strengthening and comforting to us both. I began to value these times of being alone with Ellen in the privacy of the car. I found myself trying to put into each time a small bit of shared feeling or appreciation of what our experience meant.

I began to realize that the situation was horrendous or overwhelming only in its totality, that isolated bits of the life we were living could have gem-like moments of beauty. And this was what I began to strive for and tried to communicate to Ellen.

To the times when I sensed despair in Ellen's silence, I offered fleeting yet definite gestures of love or support, wordless but clear. To the times when tears slipped silently down Ellen's cheeks, as we maneuvered homeward through freeway traffic from San Francisco, I spoke of my love for her. For us to talk about the enormity of our experience, or try to gain control and understanding of the many unknowns and imponderables which lay ahead, would be impossible. But it comforted me to put my love into words and actions at specific times and in relation to specific events. I hoped it would also bring solace to Ellen. It was a way of slicing from the unmanageable totality a small bit of experience—and then dealing effectively with it. It was the faint stumbling beginning of what was to be our way of life.

It involved total listening to Ellen's message at the specific moment of communication, and response to that message as thoughtfully and truthfully as was within my power. Sometimes I erred by responding to more than was in Ellen's message. At these times I hurt rather than helped her, and she withdrew. As the days passed, I came to see that a truthful response which answered specifically what Ellen asked, only that and no more, would bring more questions and further exploration. This was true communication, more fruitful than trying to guess at what meaning really lay behind her question and speaking to that.

In this way we were both sure that we were talking about what Ellen really wanted to deal with, and I was kept from saying things which she was not ready to hear. But there was much stumbling, and many errors. One thing alone was certain—we were in this together, totally and forever, through life and past death.

Ellen had confronted the radiotherapist with the question about being able to have a baby despite the radiation effects. He had been shocked by her apparent lack of understanding of her fate. How could she ask about having a baby when, to him, the prognosis was death—which his skill and machine might delay but not avert? Yet she asked because she wanted to believe in the future.

With me, Ellen acknowledged that the radiation had made conception impossible and then, still holding to her need for a future, she talked about ways of taking care of children who would not be her own. I honored both her feelings of loss that she could never have children of her own and her recognition that there are alternative ways of loving and serving.

To the question of the bony mass, I responded with my own belief that if the radiation therapy could make it smaller, if the transfer factor could contain the cancer and keep it from metastasis, then the doctors would surely explore further alternatives. During the spring of 1971, after radiation therapy was finished and transfer factor therapy had begun, we shared the hope that Ellen would be saved, but we acknowledged that people had died of osteogenic sarcoma.

We talked about hospitals and Ellen's feelings about the hospitalizations of her early childhood. She remembered her experiences with hatred; the thought of being hospitalized again filled her with horror.

Her fear was so great—and seemed so clearly to carry with it her reaction to the threat of being abandoned—that my response was strong and direct. "Ellen, we will never put you in the hospital, except for something that would help you to come out feeling better. And we will never put you in a hospital unless you choose to go. This is a promise."

As she began to feel better physically, gaining in weight and energy, we began to talk about living each day for itself. Whatever the final outcome, we would have some time. We would continue to direct ourselves to the quality of the time we had, knowing that none of us on this earth knew with any certainty that we had any more time than Ellen.

On rare occasions during that spring, we talked about death and its meaning for people. Ellen had never been taught religious beliefs about spiritual survival. Heaven and Hell were only words to her, to be used as expletives. In any case she had already experienced some of the quality of each here on this earth. She did have a somewhat pantheistic view of her own. She saw all life on earth as part of a greater whole. She believed that since no earthly matter is lost but is just transformed into other forms, then people who die return to the earth and are used as part of an endless chain of life, re-use, and renewal. At this point in her thinking about death in general, she seemed satisfied with the genuineness of this belief. To have believed in a more personal survival now, because she herself was threatened, would have seemed phony to her.

With some hesitance, I talked about my own experience with near-death, the lightening and peacefulness of the experience. It was clear that Ellen did not want to hear about this; she did not want to talk about it.

<h1 style="text-align:center">8</h1>

In Ellen's own deep and private thoughts, she did go beyond these discussions with me, and beyond even the thoughts she had faced in her journal.

In March she had received a letter from an old friend.

Lima, Peru
March 20, 1971

Dear Ellen,

I was in the U.S. for six weeks a week ago, and in Novato one day. Barry Miller would have driven me over to say hello, but we were already late to Berkeley by about five hours.

I don't think you have ever received any of my cards or letters and I wish I had seen you because I wanted to give you a Peruvian friendship ring in silver.

Down here now it is still summer and beautiful. Just two days ago we did have twelve cats but we gave four away to these missionary people who live in the jungle. In the jungles, "gatos" or cats are like precious treasures because they chase rats and vampire bats. I might go to the jungle, I was invited to stay at the guest-house over there by some guys that I know. Mark has lived there fifteen years and he will be eighteen soon and will be leaving.

Last summer I had lessons on the beach for horseback riding by some Italian maestro. I was given a giant black horse to use for lessons. I take these modern ballet and exercise lessons from a Frenchwoman. I was taking Hindu dance from another woman but she went back to India. Mother wants me to take Flamenco dance and start guitar again, but my other professor said I need another, since my Ecuadorian one is cracked—moving, what else.

I wish you would tell me what's happening, because I always come back so strange compared with others.

I hope to hear from you.

Luv,
Marca

Ellen tried to answer Marca's letter. In her several attempts, she was unable to deal with teenage matters. In her first letter, she went right to the heart of her devastating experience.

Novato, Calif.
April 4, 1971

Dear Marca,

I'm really, really sorry I never wrote. I got all your letters and other mail and things, but I think I just always felt so far apart from South America and you being there. I remember promising myself I'd write every week, and now I think it's been more than three years. So much has happened these past years (and it sounds like it's been the same for you) that it bowls me over to remember and get things oriented in my mind. So instead of starting at the beginning, I'll start at now.

A few months ago I discovered I had a cancerous tumor in my abdomen and am just recovering from it. I'm having severe leg pains in my right leg from the scarring of the radiation treatment. Oh God, what hell of a treatment. Thinking back on that (which

I do quite often), I thank dear God it's over and I'm alive. The leg pains don't matter and the tumor doesn't matter (it's still there and always will be) and the hell I went through doesn't matter because I'm alive and I'm strong.

These past two years my parents have been leaving each other alternately. My father had an affair and my mother stayed home and dropped tranquilizers. Jana left as soon as she could. I felt very stranded.

Now they are staying together for my sake (because of the cancer) which is the sickest of all reasons. My father has never loved my mother and it is just a very sick relationship. And like Jana I am leaving as soon as I can. It isn't that I hold the past against them (their comings and goings), they are their own persons and this is the way they choose to live their lives. It is just a very sick situation as I have said before, and I do not wish to be involved in it, and so am trying to be my own person, which is hard while living here.

Dissatisfied with what she had written, knowing she could not send this letter, yet wanting to reach out to Marca, Ellen tried again.

Dear Marca,

I have received every one of your letters and I am ashamed that I have not answered any of them. Many things have happened since you moved. Taran, my first dog, died of distemper. And so we got a second—Ralf. Ralf is a female just as Cindy is a boy. Cindy is still around. He must be 84, cat age. He's a cranky, grumpy old cat, and he slobbers a lot too. All in all, he's pretty disgusting.

For a time my parents wanted a divorce. Those years were hard for me and Jan. But now I have cancer and it probably will kill me. I have much pain. It is a solid bone tumor in my pelvic area and so far as anyone knows, there is no cure. My only hope is a sudden stop in its growth, my going into remission—I need a miracle.

At first, I could not accept death. It was impossible to me and now as time has passed, my hope becomes less and less and I begin to accept the idea of dying. It is not dying that I am afraid of. I am afraid of what pain it will bring.

And as she wrote this letter too, Ellen was dissatisfied. She made a last attempt to put her situation into words. She rewrote the last part of her letter.

In all the time between when I last knew you and now, so much has happened and I have learned a great deal from it, and I am still learning. What I want to tell you is this, that I have cancer. It is a solid bone tumor in my abdomen—still growing and it will kill me. I have much pain and sadness, but mostly I am afraid. I'm not afraid of death or what death is. What frightens me is what pain it may bring on its way.

Once this last paragraph was written, Ellen knew she could not send a letter to Marca. These were very private thoughts, and she could not share them. She put the letters into her drawer.

9

For months Ellen had talked about going east to see Dennis's store, to meet the friends Jana had told her about. She and Jana had planned to go together. Now, in April, with Jana already in Michigan, Ellen asked to go alone. The doctors agreed to the trip, and Ellen went by plane —unprotected and unsupervised—on her own.

It was a time of reunion and closeness with Jana. Dennis's parents welcomed her, and the girls had a brief taste of what life might have been like had they been able to leave home together and be on their own. Ellen felt well physically. She and Jana walked and explored together; they slept together and talked long into the night. For a brief ten days, life was what it might have been.

Ellen stopped in Illinois to see her cousin Beth and then returned home, pleased and heartened that she had undertaken and accomplished this experience which she had so wanted.

10

As spring went on, treatment with the transfer factor continued. It had become the focus of our life and everything was subordinated to its rhythm. Increasingly the pattern was colored by pain; leg and knee pain, and now pain around the tumor. Perhaps radiation scars were causing the pelvic pain. Or perhaps it was associated with increased action of lymph cells around the tumor. It seemed possible that the pain meant the transfer factor was working, though no one could say this with certainty. Ellen's rosette count was up, a good sign, and despite the pain, she continued at school. She looked forward to summer and camping trips with Troy and other friends.

That spring was a hiatus, a time of thumbing our noses at fate. The word *forever* was removed from our vocabulary. We acknowledged this, but insisted that it was so—after all—for all human beings, even though most people did not know or even give thought to life's impermanence. The word *now* dominated those days of our life. The season itself spoke of birth and rebirth and, in spite of the twinges of pain in her leg and pelvis, Ellen felt well.

For me, this shift from *always* to *now* was a major change in my thinking. It reached into the Achilles heel of my clinging-clutching pattern of behavior toward David and Jana. With Ellen, the clutching had always been less of a problem. Perhaps because of her early physical difficulties, my reaching-out and holding-on had been truly supportive, and the relationship had become a more fully reciprocal one.

Now as I went about routine tasks, I found myself speaking aloud, telling myself that if I could give up *forever* and *always* in regard to Ellen, I could do the same with others, too. I settled for *now*, cherishing my hope for tomorrow but acknowledging that tomorrow might not include Ellen. And I engraved the moments of *now* of that spring in my memory and my heart, aware that I might have to carry them as my strength and resource in all the days and months to come.

For Ellen, the emphasis was on putting into her life *now* the experiences and relationships of lasting and eternal value. It was no longer possible to settle for the impermanent, temporary, or unimportant. She ended many of her letters to Jana, sent and unsent, with—"I'm Alive!" The dross, the unimportant detail fell away, revealing the pure gold of her depth. And so together in this seemingly contradictory manner we lived our days.

This shift and growth would have been impossible without Ellen's doctors. They were complete opposites in manner. Dr. Alton: dignified, patient, careful in his words, honest yet compassionate, with years of practice and specialization behind him, learned yet ever-learning about his craft and about people; Dr. Lorin: deliberately challenging all the shibboleths of established medical practitioners, deliberately unorthodox in appearance, manner and speech, yet gentle and profoundly caring in his relationship with Ellen. Together he and Ellen damned or laughed at small things and people, while with absolute seriousness, intensity, and care, they challenged their enemy—the sarcoma.

The doctors worked together. Dr. Alton believed in Dr. Lorin's work. He recognized it as perhaps the most important new frontier in cancer treatment. He acknowledged that the way ahead was into unexplored territory, but he was willing, as we were, to participate in the charting. In our talks together, Dr. Alton reminded me that our chances were slim, since metastasis might well have occurred even though it did not show on the x-rays. He would sigh. "All it takes is one cancer cell in the blood stream."

At those times, the cry within me for *always* and *forever* would return and protest, "Don't tell me she will die. Don't mourn with me." But as I left his office, the growing ability to live *now* would return and take over. My thoughts were a silent shout: "I'm not ready to mourn. I'll take *now*. No one knows if they have any more than *now* anyway!"

In my talks with Dr. Alton, I was able to express the purely selfish meaning Ellen had in my personal existence. Ellen was the pearl, the glimpse of the near-perfection of love in my life. She was also the link that kept the family together. It was well-nigh impossible for me to envision our life without her.

And what of David and his relationship with Ellen and with me? Clearly the relationship with Ellen was primary. He gave his blood to save her; he would also have gladly given his life.

The coexistence between David and me was careful and considerate. We were intimate strangers with the same goal—saving Ellen's life. We accepted the shared burden. For me, the words *with grace* took on new meaning. I told myself that since life's tasks must be lived out, let it be with grace.

Ellen knew that we were together as our gift to her. She

protested it—she did not want us to stay together for her. If we were to remain together as a family, let it be because we loved each other, too.

At this point, love between David and me was not possible. But stay together we did, striving in total cooperation to meet the stresses of Ellen's illness and to save her life.

11

We were all living a delicate balance of love and forbearance, of hope and realization of the deadly illness, of acceptance of the terms of present life and defiance of ultimate defeat. In addition, for Ellen and me, there was just the beginning of a recognition of death's benign aspects balanced against a grasp of life's deep and permanent values. Ellen's apparent physical well-being was the fulcrum upon which the balance rested. Late in May, as the school year drew to a close, the balance crashed.

Ellen and Troy had gone on a weekend camp-out in the neighboring hills. The excursion ended disastrously in chilling and total exhaustion for Ellen. She crept down from the mountainside, dry-eyed, almost wordless. It had been a nightmare of trying to be what she had effortlessly been before—only to find that she could no longer climb hills, or keep going in search of a perfect campsite, or sleep on the hard ground in her sleeping bag: perfectly ordinary activities, but she could no longer do them.

With the exhaustion came extreme pain and depression. Dr. Lorin reported that Ellen's rosette count was down. She had used herself up; all reserves were gone. She spent days flat on her back. When she started to get around again, she found to her deep discouragement that the leg pain and weakness forced her to use crutches. She ended the school year on crutches, answering the well-meaning queries of acquaintances with flippancy.

"A horse stepped on my foot."

Her friends knew she had cancer.

IV

1971: SUMMER
Loss

I looked up at the blue sky
It said hello
I felt the sun shine
It warmed my soul.
It felt warm, it felt warm, it felt warm.
I felt the wind blow against my nose
It spoke very softly and whispered good day.
Good day, good day, to everyone good day,
I'll be on my way.

Troy — *Words to*
a song for flute and guitar

1

If spring had been a time of assertion, of hope and life, summer was a time of loss. The turning point had been the late spring camp-out. Ellen had now lost freedom of movement. It was a bitter loss. The crutches were a hated symbol and she still tried desperately to get along without them.

She also began to lose her comparative freedom from pain and pain-control medication. It became necessary to explore various analgesics, to seek for combinations which would ease the pain, yet leave her mind and spirit undulled. The sources of the pain were much in question. Dr. Lorin believed that the transfer factor triggered an increase in pain at the tumor site because, in mobilizing Ellen's own body resources against the cancer cells, the action of lymph cells was increased where the tumor was located. Swelling occurred which impinged upon nerves. Flashes and messages of pain were experienced all up and down that lower right quadrant of her body.

But there was another, more ominous, possibility: that the doctors were no longer "on top of" the illness, that the tumor was growing again, but that it did not show up on the x-rays. If so, the tumor growth itself was responsible for the increased pain.

In June, Jana and Dennis returned from Michigan. They had given up their store and were ready now to stay in California. They joined a group of other young people living in a cooperative setting and became involved in community work, newspaper writing, and wholesale food purchasing and distributing. Their purpose was to combat the private enterprise system which they regarded as corrupt and archaic. They tried to make services such as their 'food conspiracy' available to people who wished to lower their food costs. They fought the city council of their town in trying to get a meeting place for young people. The community itself was divided in its opinions of them and their efforts.

Soon after Jana returned, she sought out Dr. Alton. She asked him direct questions and listened to his answers. Yes, aided by the crutches and the pain-medication, Ellen seemed moderately comfortable. Yes, this was better than the doctors had expected. Yes, the transfer factor seemed to be helping her to feel better, though perhaps the radiation therapy really had helped more than we, her family, would acknowledge. No, the transfer factor had never yet saved anyone's life. Yes, Ellen would probably die because of the cancer. No, he did not know how long Ellen would live. After this meeting with Dr. Alton, Jana did not again press me to keep Ellen's imminent death in the front of our thoughts as we made our day-to-day choices.

Ellen yearned to be part of the life in their collective. But though she spent many days and nights with them, she was limited by her own pain and their inability to provide special arrangements for her. Reluctantly, she accepted the fact that her ability to participate fully in their life was a lost cause.

The relationship with Troy was temporarily lost that summer. He and another friend went East to live and work with relatives. It was necessary for him to find himself as a person again, apart from his involvement with Ellen. Denial of her illness would no longer work.

Ellen went with his family to the airport to see him off. He was gone all that summer. Of his ambivalent feelings about leaving, a letter spoke in understatement.

Wyeville, Wisconsin
June 28, 1971
Dear El,

I have just gotten up to see the sunrise. Matt and I slept outside and everything is beautiful. I really felt bad about not really saying goodbye. We made it by a whole hour and 45 minutes, and still, sure enough, we had to run down the hallway to catch the plane. I felt like I wanted to run off the plane, but the engines started and there we were. My flight was alright until it got over Chicago. There was a thunderstorm that threw the plane all over.

Visiting my home town was strange, as I thought it would be. It seemed like the town had changed and yet it was the same. It's really me that did the changing. My friends didn't know how to talk to me as a friend. It was like I had just moved into the town that I had never been to but had dreamed about. And it was exactly how I had dreamed it to be.

Troy

In her fight against pain and medication, Ellen began to lose contact with other friends. Sensing that her experiences were taking her beyond the range of understanding of other young people, Ellen extended her efforts to maintain her friendships. She found other girls preoccupied with teen-age interests: driver-training, boys and the intricacies of boy-girl games, summer jobs, clothing. The list was endless, but because she had valued and still clung to her friendships with these girls, Ellen tried to share what she could with them.

With Lurene, her 'best' friend from junior high school days, she shared an interest in music. Lurene had bought a flute with her earnings from long afternoons and evenings of work at a local hamburger joint. Ellen undertook to teach her to play the flute and they spent many afternoons together with their music.

David and I encouraged the friendship; we tried to arrange for experiences which they had previously shared and enjoyed. One bright day in June we went to the ocean: Lurene and her dog, Ellen and her dog Ralf, David and I. It was a golden day, without fog or haze, windless, comfortably warm. The dogs raced across the sand, crashing into the water and out again, running back to us, trampling across the blankets where we sat, vigorously shaking water and sand on us. In self-defense, to tame this boundless energy, the girls leashed the dogs and walked, Ellen limping as she favored her leg, Ralf pulling her along the wet sand, as the water foamed in wavelets on their bare feet.

Despite the still pleasurable experiences with Ellen, Lurene was going on with the unfolding of her own healthy life. The ability to drive a car opened up new worlds for her, the responsibilities and income from her part-time job brought her experiences which Ellen could not share. We felt this, as Ellen did, and it was painful.

Judy, another friend from earlier childhood days, had also entered the world of the sixteen-year-old. Long girl-talk afternoons were no longer an important part of her life. The small adventures of childhood exploration she and Ellen had shared were no longer enough for a sustained relationship and Ellen could not share Judy's new interests except as a listener.

For Ellen these hurts were as painful emotionally as her illness was physically. Both Lurene and Judy could have dealt supportively with a brief intense illness, for they had been Ellen's good friends. But this long, drawn-out malady was more than they could bear. Both girls alternately offered and withdrew friendship. Ellen understood, perhaps more than they did themselves, and was hurt.

In July, Ellen made another desperate attempt to keep her own freedom of movement. She arranged to go camping with friends—a married couple with two small daughters, friends for whom she had baby-sat in earlier days. She grudgingly accepted the need for crutches and pain pills. She promised to eat and sleep and rest. She entreated her doctors to let her go. With misgivings, they agreed. She left by car with her friends, triumphant, determined that she would force her body to serve her and allow her this experience.

After about a week spent at pre-arranged campsites in Southern California, it became clear to Ellen and the others that enjoyment had turned into endurance, that it was not possible to control the pain under these somewhat primitive living conditions. Defeated, they put Ellen on a plane and she flew home, while they completed the trip. It was Ellen's admission of defeat and loss. Her spirit could no longer force her body to obey. When she returned home, she wrote of this and other losses to Lurene.

Dear Lu,

I didn't feel like calling you, mostly because I don't know what to say. But I felt like talking to you. I'm back from camping. It didn't really work out. I ended up flying home a week early because of my fucking leg. The people down in Southern California are really unfriendly. They all came in their little groups and they all stayed in their little groups and the only time anyone really answered my hello was for a pickup. Why the fuck can't a person say hello to another, when it concerns one of the opposite sex, without it being taken as, "Hey babe wanta go for a ride?" Holy Shit.

We keep saying, "Hey we got to get out and do something together," when the truth is

Here Ellen broke off this letter, and started over.

Dear Lu,

I didn't feel like calling but I felt like talking to you. One-way conversations are the best sometimes. I'm back from camping. It didn't really work out but the week I was there was really fun. I ended up flying home. I went skinny dipping way down on the beach where no one was, it was so fantastic to swim in the ocean. You'd come up for a breath of air and a wave would come down and smash you or you'd be swimming and the undertow would catch you as a wave would come over you and grind you into the sand. But the sea was really fantastic.

Later we went to the mountains and that was really fun. It was right before the 4th of July weekend and the camp area was pretty empty. So all the raccoons and squirrels scarfed off us. It was beautiful. They came up and ate right out of your hand. We fed them good stuff like marshmallows and chocolate chip cookies. God, I think they eat anything. We woke up in the middle of the night and found our garbage ripped to pieces by the little buggers. Troy went back east to see his cousin. I think I told you already. Anyway, he'll probably be gone all summer. Ahhh—

These letters were never sent. They joined the letters to Marca in Ellen's drawer.

2

Sensing the intensity of her defeat, and recognizing Ellen's need to control her own body in dealing with the pain and increasing disability, David arranged for sessions in self-hypnosis. Ellen was dubious, reluctant, chagrined, but also desperate. So it was with ambivalent feelings that the relationship with Dr. Danby began. He was a long-time friend of David's, a specialist in internal medicine, who several years before had been severely injured in a car accident. He had spent long months hospitalized with many broken bones, and then many more months severely limited by pain as he mended slowly. Refusing to accept the prospect of permanent traumatic arthritis, he had explored the avenue of self-hypnosis to control the pain and compel his body to do his bidding. For himself, he had found the path of self-hypnosis a useful adjunct to his medical knowledge—a means of reducing his limitations and enlarging his physical and perhaps emotional boundaries. At David's request now, and with the consent of Ellen's doctors, he brought this skill to Ellen.

Her doubts gave way and she followed him along this avenue, totally new to her. He moved rapidly through his own hypnotism of her—doing just enough to show her it could be done, not enough to give her a feeling of being subject to or dominated by him. His emphasis was on teaching Ellen to hypnotize herself, using her own mind to block out and overcome the messages of pain it was receiving. He supported both Ellen and David in their dislike for the pain-killing drugs which were becoming so much a part of her life. He sought to help her develop the strength of mind and will which would make heavy medication unnecessary—at least for now.

For a time that summer David and Dr. Danby tried to put the self-hypnosis on a more objective, less family-friend basis. They arranged for a skilled professional hypnotist to work with Ellen. This man was also a physician, a specialist in obstetrics, who found hypnotism—and self-hypnosis by patients—a useful method in dealing with the pain of childbirth. His compassion aroused, he tried to help Ellen.

Unfortunately, his treatment harmed rather than helped Ellen. In a lengthy session with her, during which he had directed her back to one of her very early experiences of corrective surgery, he was called to another office by a sudden emergency, leaving Ellen still under hypnosis. He returned to find her frantic, nearly hysterical, and thereafter totally unforgiving toward him.

Hypnotized, having given up her own control, she had been re-experiencing a time when she had been left in a hospital to face anesthesia and post-operative pain—a time when, too young to understand reasons or explanations, she had felt deserted. Now under hypnosis, she was again deserted. He had reinforced her fear of being abandoned. Ellen refused to cooperate any further with this doctor. She went

back just one more time to see him and tell him of her anger
toward him.

So Fred Danby again took up the charge of easing
Ellen's present pain. He sought to help her retain control
over her body and also to provide her with a tool which
would help ease her fear of the future.

3

In late July, we learned of another loss. Dr. Alton was
going abroad, to England and France, to study and learn
more about cancer treatment. The emphasis in London was
on new drugs and their combinations. He planned to spend
several months there. Then he would go on to Paris where
pioneering work in immunology was being carried on. He
planned to be in Europe for ten months, until June 1972.

Dr. Alton told me of his plans while Ellen was out of
the examining room for a few minutes. Undoubtedly, he
chose to tell me and to prepare me first, so that I could help
Ellen when she returned.

I listened; my feeling of loss was so great that I felt
numb. I could not react. I responded stiffly and politely,
"That's very nice. Be sure to let us know if you learn of
anything that could help Ellen."

I tried to tell myself that this was a stroke of luck, that
it would substitute for a search of our own through other
medical centers for new approaches, new cures. But within
me raged the accusation, "You said you'd be here. You said
you'd see us through!" And the desperate unvoiced question, "How will we manage without you?"

Aware perhaps of my distress, Dr. Alton told me about
another doctor—an associate in treating childhood

cancer—Dr. Kramer. He would take over Ellen's care. This doctor knew Dr. Lorin, too, and the two doctors would work together. Dr. Alton spoke also of a new facet to Ellen's treatment, decided upon in consultation with the other doctors. Because of Ellen's dropping rosette count and the concern that perhaps there was a flagging in David's ability to confer immunological boosting to Ellen's own immune system, they wished to start innoculating her with something called "BCG." It was being used in Paris and a few other treatment centers and would be given to Ellen like smallpox vaccinations. Dr. Lorin would use it in combination and alternation with the transfer factor.

Very soon my private moment with the doctor was over. Ellen was back and it was time to tell her of the coming changes. For both of us, June 1972 could have been an eternity away. There was no way of putting into words our sense of loss. When we left the office that day, I felt certain that Ellen would not be alive when Dr. Alton returned.

Later, when I joined Ellen in a session with Frances, the bitter tears came over this loss which felt so much like desertion. Frances suggested, "Maybe you should tell him how you feel." Perhaps Ellen would. For myself, I shook my head.

"It's no use. He has to go his way."

And I went then to call Dr. Kramer's office for an appointment, so that the transition could be made.

V

1971: AUTUMN
Search

*I must launch out my boat. The languid
hours pass by on the shore—Alas for me!
 The spring has done its flowering and
taken leave. And now with the burden of
faded futile flowers I wait and linger.
 The waves have become clamorous,
and upon the bank in the shady lane
the yellow leaves flutter and fall.
 What emptiness do you gaze upon!
Do you not feel a thrill passing through
the air with the notes of the far away
song floating from the other shore?*

Rabindranath Tagore, *Gitanjali, 21*

1

With the start of the BCG, hope returned. Ellen's body
showed clear response to the innoculations, indicating that
her immune system was reacting. Dr. Lorin, somewhat
dubious at first about combining the two treatments, was
delighted when Ellen developed a rash-like reaction to the
vaccinations. He took this to indicate an improvement in
her body's faulty system of recognizing foreign matter.

With renewed vigor he stepped up the pace of the treatment. The rosette count went up. The weakness and pain decreased. He talked again about getting on top of the illness.

Contact had already been established with Dr. Kramer. We found his style of relating to Ellen very different from Dr. Alton's. Dr. Alton had spent long sessions with Ellen exploring questions and answers, inviting her confidences about her non-medical activities—sometimes while the office waiting room was crowded with other less gravely ill patients.

Dr. Kramer operated on a tight schedule. More and more as the weekly appointments passed, we thought of him as a sleek, handsome, meticulously-maintained train, operating on a pre-arranged timetable. Clearly he did not wish to discuss Ellen's feelings about her illness. He supervised the treatment competently. But with an already large practice of his own, he seemed to feel burdened by the additional load of Dr. Alton's leukemia and cancer patients.

To both Ellen and me, it sometimes seemed that we came away from these appointments with only 'pain pill' prescriptions or x-ray orders. No human transaction had taken place. On those days our drive home from San Francisco would be silent.

Finally Ellen said, "It wasn't worth the hassle to go all the way into San Francisco for that." And so we began to go to this doctor less frequently, and he seemed satisfied with the arrangement. He prescribed medicines in sufficient quantities to last through the intervals between office visits.

Perhaps sensing the distance between this new doctor and Ellen, Dr. Lorin took on a more emotionally supportive role. One Friday afternoon in late September, he telephoned, controlled excitement in his voice.

"Can you come down to the lab now? There's someone I want you to meet."

We went, of course, and met a young woman, a physician at the university hospital. Dr. Lorin had learned, in the course of other professional dealings, that when she was younger, she too had a sarcoma—though not a bone producing one—located in her pelvic area. She was, after numerous operations, now alive and well and practicing medicine. So much for predictions that all sarcomas brought death.

In that crowded, seemingly chaotic but beehive-like organized laboratory, Dr. Roberts sat quietly and talked with Ellen about her own experiences; the pain of numerous operations, the fear and uncertainty about the illness, the thankfulness for each day of living. Soberly Ellen listened. She nodded. Together this young woman and the girl, not yet a woman, shared their feelings about the terrible confrontation with this illness.

Dr. Roberts made clear her wish to contribute transfer factor for Ellen; Dr. Lorin was delighted. What better donor than a person who had recovered from cancer?

As we drove home, I truly felt that Ellen had been rescued. Dr. Roberts's offer seemed an omen, a promise that Ellen would get well. Ellen smiled and lay back resting. She broke her silence to say, "I would never have met any of these people if I hadn't gotten sick. I think I'm not sorry."

Sadly for us, a week later Dr. Roberts withdrew her offer. We were told that she had learned she could not give blood to Ellen because she had once had hepatitis. I wondered: how could a physician have been unaware of this complication when she first made her offer? But even though we said, "We'll take our chances with the hepatitis," the offer remained withdrawn. More painful than an offer never made. Dr. Lorin was chagrined, disappointed.

He began to play what he called 'musical surgeons.' With the rosette count up again he felt he might persuade a skilled surgeon to remove part of the cancerous bony tumor. He was not advocating amputation—that was not possible because of the location of Ellen's tumor. He was trying to get its size reduced, in hope that he could then inject transfer factor directly into what remained of the tumor.

With Dr. Kramer's acquiescence rather than support, Dr. Lorin arranged for a consultation with a surgeon at the university hospital. The doctors examined Ellen, who was resentful and frightened again. Then while Frances remained with Ellen to comfort her, the doctors met with David, Jana and me.

Busy men, they could not take the time to find an empty conference room. So we stood in the corridor, while the surgeon explained in detached remote tones that, given the site of Ellen's tumor, he could see no way of performing surgery. He would not accept Dr. Lorin's suggestion of partial removal of the tumor. No, no, that would only hasten metastasis, and the x-rays already now showed a tiny spot on her left lung.

It was like a death sentence—metastasis had taken place, and no one had told us until this moment. Now this stranger was withholding his skills because he believed she could not be saved and should be spared mutilating surgery. For me, hope of saving Ellen's life ended that day in October, during this hurried meeting in the hospital corridor. Dr. Kramer brought the conference to a close.

"I must run. My appointments are waiting for me. Call me if you want to talk further."

2

David embarked again on his own desperate search—he had heard that laser beams were being used to treat cancer at another university hospital in Northern California. Would Dr. Kramer explore this possibility? Courteously, detachedly, the doctor did so, and returned the information that the medical authorities at the hospital had advised that the laser beam technique would not work for Ellen.

So Ellen's treatment remained in Dr. Lorin's hands. He believed that as long as he could keep her rosette count up, he would delay further metastasis. But he was powerless to remove the primary tumor.

Ellen remained unaware of much of this. She had been furious when she was left with Frances, excluded from that October conference. And now, since there were no new decisions to be made, it seemed fruitless to share the negative responses with her. She had already been deeply disappointed by Dr. Roberts' withdrawal.

Meanwhile, through a friend of Jana's we met Mary Morgan who had gained recognition in the San Francisco area for her ability to teach meditation and for some healing powers. In her public lectures and on television programs she had also told of several out-of-the-body experiences.

We went to her public lectures. Troy, who had returned from his trip East, went with us. As we listened, we were impressed by Mary's sincerity and obvious desire to help people deal with the difficulties and uncertainties of their lives. We sat in the smoke-filled church used as an auditorium and watched the interaction between the audience and Mary, who was on a small stage at the front of the hall, her tremendous warmth and magnetism reaching out to all of us. There was frivolity and evident selfishness in some of the questions put to Mary from the audience. Troy and Ellen reacted to the atmosphere of tension and grasping for personal predictions which seemed to pervade the audience.

In a note to Ellen, Troy commented,

She seems to be wanting to be a psychic healer and to do good things for people. That is fine, but why must she answer ridiculous questions? Why not stay with plain meditation and forget the predictions? I think it would be much better; it may not draw crowds, but at least she would be being truthful—which she seems to be after. People need something to believe in and to cling to.

Ellen answered,

People seem to ask ridiculous questions—use her as a medium. They come for predictions. They ask very personal questions to test her. Why does she answer? Does she see them as testing her?

Tentatively, after one such lecture, we approached Mary, not really knowing what we could ask or what she could offer. Jana's friend had already told her about Ellen, and when we approached her she directed us to a weekly meditation group. She also offered to meet with Ellen at her own home.

In her home she saw a number of cancer patients, without any fee, in individual and group meetings. She tried to use her energy to reduce their pain and strengthen their fight against the illness—directing her psychic energy to their tumor sites.

Again we were in uncharted waters. We turned to Mary because of her sincerity and warmth—and because we were desperate. Drawn to Ellen, who had known her own eighteen-year-old son before his untimely death in Vietnam, Mary gave freely of her time and energy. For more than a month, during September and early October, she spent almost nightly sessions with Ellen, placing her gifted hands on the tumor site, willing it to diminish and to cease causing pain. Her other focus with Ellen was to teach the girl how to meditate and draw on her own positive energy resources.

David, Jana and Troy were skeptical. Ellen was dubious at first; then convinced that she felt the emanation of energy and comfort from Mary's hands. Dr. Danby, who was continuing his supportive contact with Ellen, could see no harm in our work with Mary. I doubted the possibility of healing but felt that the meditation was good. In any case, during the month when Ellen saw Mary, she felt quite well, with greater energy and less pain.

The relationship with Mary could not continue on an intensive level. Too many other desperate people wanted slices of her time and energy. She tapered off her contacts with Ellen, admonishing her, "Keep meditating, kiddo. That's your way of life."

3

Meanwhile, the practical mundane details of daily living had to be worked out. After long talks with Jana and Ellen, I decided to return to my teaching job that September. There were several considerations: I felt a desperate need for financial self-sufficiency since a "husband working—wife at home" status did not fit with what there was of this marriage; I had great personal need for the positive feedback from children, parents, and colleagues; and, perhaps most important, Jana had offered to return home to live if she could be truly useful. Jana did not want to live with us as just an occasional substitute for me. She said she wanted to carry the primary responsibility for Ellen's care during the weekdays. She would regard it as her job, taking weekends and some evenings off.

The timing of the beginning of the school year fit in with Jana's own personal situation. Living in the collective situation had become filled with strains and difficulties and she was also trying to end what she called her monogamous relationship with Dennis. She was looking outward and becoming interested in other people. It seemed likely that Dennis would soon return to Michigan, and this time she did not want to go with him.

So Jana moved back home. Together she and Ellen looked forward to many shared experiences. We bought a small car so that Jana could take Ellen to and from the two classes for which Ellen had registered at the high school. The car also gave the girls mobility for pleasure drives and for the weekly sessions with Frances in San Francisco.

David and I would continue to take Ellen to the appointments with Dr. Kramer. David would continue to give blood for the transfer factor. We would all share the responsibility of getting Ellen to the Hematology Lab for her shots and innoculations with Dr. Lorin.

Ellen was pleased with the arrangement. It was September; she was seeing both Mary Morgan and Fred Danby, practicing meditation and self-hypnosis. She felt relatively free from pain. Troy was back. She hoped to again pick up her friendships at school. And most important, Jana would be with her.

Her spirits high, determined to maintain her freedom of movement, she wrote to Beth.

Novato, California
September 18, 1971

Dear Beth,

Here are the rice paper prints I made. They're beautiful when you hold them up to the sun. Maybe you could tape them to your window.

I'm on crutches mostly now—and carrying books got kind of difficult, so I got myself a small backpack. I just throw everything in it and throw it across my back, and I'm off and hobbling!

All my love,
El

4

At the beginning of that school year, Jana and Ellen began to keep a journal together in which they wrote feelings and thoughts which they wanted to share.

September 1, 1971

Writing in this notebook—is like being able to express thoughts and feelings, anything I want to say. I say now—this is a sheet of paper—just like any old sheet of paper—but soon you will have ME on you!

Ellen

We will write what we want! Yeah! The freedom of the pen!

Jana

Several weeks after Jana returned home, the collective broke up completely and some young people were left without a place to live. At Jana's request, two young men, Tim and Cary, came to live with us until they could find other housing. The prospect of having a communal arrangement pleased Ellen, David was neutral, and I quieted my misgivings by telling myself it would be a help in meeting Jana's need for company and Ellen's need for care and support.

As it turned out, this experience became a trial by fire for all of us. The young men stayed several months; they were intent on their own political and social activities, pulling Jana in their direction rather than helping and supporting her in the job she had taken on. There was enmity between Tim and Dennis, who had gone to live in Berkeley. Jana found herself juggling her relationships with two jealous young men and a sick sister. Some of the entries in the shared journal tell of this problem.

Sept. 5, 1971

Jan,

You didn't come. You didn't show up. You just stayed in Berkeley with Dennis. I feel like I'm pulling just as hard on you but at the same time I'm really mad at you. I feel like you forgot about me, or Dennis kept saying to you, "Jan, stay, stay," or something like that happened.

But I don't want to turn you into a piece of play-doh. That's what I see Dennis doing to you. I really don't know your relationship with Tim, but I see you pulled all over. But I'm mad because you said you'd be there and you weren't! I wanted your company. I just wanted you to be there.

El

Sept. 6

Dear Ellen,

I am sorry that I was not there to keep you company. My only excuse is that I am unclear as to exactly what I am doing. I don't really know what my plans are. In the future I will try to be more clear in my actions.

Jan

Jan,

You don't have to make clear to me all the time what you're doing and where. At least I don't want to do that to you. You are your own person and no one can take that from you. That's what I always keep in mind or try to—like at school, it keeps me strong.

El

Sept. 7

El,

Keeping in mind that you are your own person keeps you strong?

Jan

Sept. 7

Jan,

Right on.

El

Sept. 8

El,

Does your keeping your own and another person's separate personhood in mind keep you from being possessive? Also—my being clear in my actions enables you to be less possessive—no?

Jan

Sept. 8

Jan,

True to the latter. But I don't understand what you said before. What did you say?

El

Sept. 9

El,

Just that I think possibly the fact that you were mad at me is due to feeling jealous. When you counter that with feeling that I

*am my own person, who loves you even when I am not with you, no
more feelings of possessiveness. Then I realized that you hold on to
something when you are not sure of it, and if I made myself clear as
to what time I would be away from you, you could be sure of
me—See?*

Jan

Sept. 12

Jan,

*You're right—I do agree. Many times I do feel very possessive of
you. I see that I am contradicting myself in saying those two
things.*

*School tomorrow—Blaaah. Hope it's good. But I can make it
good for myself. Right now I feel strong. I don't have to "keep up
with the crowd" at lunch break. I can read or do my art or even
homework. My choice for going to school was to take a few courses
to learn because I want to. But also to be able to have a time when I
can relate to people my own age which is important to me. But I
don't have to push myself to keep up with the people for fear of losing
them. How can you lose people? Well—lose contact in relating with
them, to them. That's my fear. I wonder am I going to have to be
the one constantly pushing to keep the channels open with them. I
don't have that energy. I feel Lurene's gone away, or else I've—I
don't know.*

El

Sept. 12

El,

*I guess you just said—in other words—what I was trying to say
to you about the pain, and the illness. When the pain demands
your attention, how can you struggle with school and people too? I
am sorry that school is equivalent to seeing people. The suffering*

involved in struggling with the cancer—people—and school will be great if you don't make priorities and stick by them.

Jan

Sept. 15

Jan,

When there is fear, there is no love. Along with fear comes distrust, suspicion, hate. With the absence of fear you have freedom—love. What is life—it is such a complex thing and yet at the same time so simple—it's silly to pin a definition on it. If you can understand all these complex things—fear, freedom, love—and still at the same time keep your mind simple—and love the beauty of a sunny day, just because it's a sunny day—then you can truly be free.

El

Sept. 20, 1971

Jan,

Came to some thoughts tonight, after the meeting, which I have been trying to put together for a week. One thing, people are all looking for the highest point, the one that will bring peace of mind. They came to the meeting (with Mary Morgan)—thinking—maybe this is the way. Or some are even just paying their two dollars to get their fortune told. They ask personal questions and some very personal—to test her (Mary) out? To find the answer? They seem so silly and shallow. But Mary really feels she must answer these questions. She really feels that she has or was given a gift. The gift of healing or being psychic and that she is meant to pass on what she can to other people no matter how petty the question. The thing that I can't accept is the spirits, the guides, the entities knocking around the room and the surrounding yourself in the white light for protection. This isn't what I'm looking for. I'm looking for—I'm looking for peace of mind just as every one else. But I have cancer.

I'm sick, and it just doesn't seem to be the answer now—maybe never. I'm still as confused as I was a week ago. The meditation group seemed empty for me in the way they all have pat answers, memorized answers and it seemed shallow. I feel meditation is very good. It's a very peaceful thing for mind and soul, spirit. But what is the reason for having a set schedule, making stronger "vibes" they say, for heightening your level after lots of practice. I feel totally disgusted with them—the people in the group. But I'm willing to try it again, I think, if only to clarify my reason for not going.

El

Sept. 21

El,

　What is confusing you so much? The correct method for finding peace of mind or what?

　Don't be too angry at these people for misunderstanding Mary. They aren't desperate.

Jan

5

With Troy's return from his trip, he and Ellen picked up their friendship again. In early fall, when Ellen seemed again to be on top of the illness, the two participated in outside activities. They shared in publishing a newspaper called *Free Youth*. It was disapproved of by the school authorities, which made it all the more attractive. Ellen and Troy shared responsibility for the artwork in the newspaper—he, by virtue of his excellent artistic ability, she, because she wanted to help him. She also carefully and painstakingly wrote some articles stating her position on students' rights.

October, 1971

I've been hearing that there are a lot of complaints about this paper Free Youth *by different school administrators.*

I suppose this is because of its promotion of Planned Parenthood and Draft Counseling for people of our age. In other words, because of its openness to us.

I feel the youth in this country are very oppressed and need to be heard. No matter how gross or crude our ideas and problems appear to be, they need to be expressed and the problem helped.

Many students want a say in what is happening in this county. They want a share in the decision-making position.

As it is now may students have no idea of what is going on; many don't care.

One question I have is whether the hills are going to be torn to shreds and turned into apartment buildings for as far as the eye can see or be left to heal over the damage that has already been done to them. The youth want a say on which way it goes.

When I personally go to these meetings on further building, I come out feeling confused, unexpressed, and unheard. The council has talked around everyone.

I feel the only way of reaching this goal is getting young people together on different subjects coming up on the agendas and forming youth organizations with representatives to represent us and our views. The students need to get organized and informed. One way of accomplishing this is publicizing our position(s) hoping more people will come to the meetings and join or support us on our positions.

Ellen

November, 1971

It is very clear to me that the parents in this county, who elect all the administrators and the Boards of Education, don't give a damn about knowledge. All they seem to be concerned with is the grades that are brought home and the little piece of paper—the diploma that says this certain student has fulfilled the requirements and has graduated from this High School. Are grades such a true symbol of a student's learning?

We are taught (programmed) from our youngest years in school that this is what is good and this is what is wanted. How do we cut ourselves off from this programming when we still have this grade system, when our parents still expect it of us? I don't know exactly what should take its place, but definitely something that doesn't turn us into robots grasping for a ridiculous symbol—a grade. I see it as not only there having to be a change in the evaluation system, but also a change in the students. We are going to have to say it's time to pull away from the present system and stop caring about how we are evaluated. How can you evaluate what someone has gained in the way of knowledge? It is no longer true what they have always told us: "It's not what we give you, it's what you've earned." This could only apply to written work or assignments.

I feel that teachers are beginning to change in their way of teaching as it is hard to grade with a system that is becoming obsolete.

Ellen

6

Early autumn turned toward winter; the BCG and transfer factor treatment continued with Dr. Lorin. Dr. Kramer continued to supervise the other medical and pain-control problems as Ellen began to experience marked increase in pain. She now needed the crutches almost constantly. She could no longer manage without a tight schedule of pain medication. She needed careful planning and transportation for any outside activity.

Added to the leg and pelvic pain, she began to have difficulty and pain in elimination and urination. Dr. Kramer referred Ellen to a urologist who had worked closely with Dr. Alton on previous occasions. Here, in this new office, we again experienced deep compassion and caring. The urologist recommended kidney and bladder function tests. These were exacting tests, since they would try to determine if the tumor had begun to displace the internal organs to a point where their function was impaired.

Ellen listened, and then we left with written instructions, for the tests required some difficult and unpleasant preparations at home the day before, and an appointment slip. As we drove home, the tears and questions came.

"What can they do about the tumor regardless of what they find?"

"Nothing about the tumor, but they can prescribe medicine to ease the problem."

It was the next day that Ellen reached a decision. She would not take the tests. This doctor could not correct the basic cause. If the tumor was growing and pushing organs out of place, he could not stop it. The urologist would have to prescribe medicines to ease the symptoms without her going through the hassle of tests. For the first time, Ellen said no to a medical procedure; we understood and accepted her decision, and the doctor tried to help her anyway.

7

The weeks went by. Almost a year had passed since the diagnosis. The pain continued to become more intense; Ellen found it increasingly difficult to get around even with crutches.

It was a dismal late afternoon in mid-December. Ellen and I had dragged ourselves into San Francisco for our appointment with Dr. Kramer. He was radiating pre-holiday cheer, but as always, his examination of Ellen was impersonal and cursory. It suddenly seemed very important to Ellen and to me that we talk with him, right there and then, about Ellen's illness and her feelings about it. It was important that he know how we felt about him. It was a painful confrontation: we made clear that we saw his methods as impersonal and cool, though not unkind, that he seemed focused on his own schedule rather than on his patient's needs—and therefore his attitude was depersonalizing to Ellen.

The doctor listened. It seemed to us that he really listened. He then clarified his situation: he could not put aside his need to keep to a punctual schedule of short appointments. But he offered to be available to us for any evening consultation and for help by telephone at any hour of the day or night. We left, feeling that we had found the human being under the ultra-efficient exterior. And he kept his word, coming through time and again for us during the next painful months.

8

One Sunday afternoon, late in December, Dr. Alton telephoned us from London. He was responding to a letter which David had written after that terrible conference with the surgeon in October, asking him to call if he knew of any possible new treatment for Ellen. As always, hope rose, only to be put down again, as Dr. Alton told about the treatment and research situation in London.

The emphasis there was on drugs or chemotherapy. Like the drugs used in the United States, they were not curative; they could only suppress the body's ineffective immune system and take over the task of killing cancer cells. The mathematics and rhythms of cancer cell production were such that no drug, not even the newest, could kill all the malignant cells. The new drugs, like those already considered and rejected for Ellen last year, were highly toxic. Serious side effects could result. Further, these drugs could not be used with the transfer factor and BCG, since chemotherapy suppressed the body's own immune system, while Dr. Lorin's immunology treatment encouraged the body's defenses against the illness.

So yet another avenue of hope was closed.

9

Another telephone call was made in late December —this time to a nurse whose name had been given to us almost casually by Dr. Kramer. He said, "Anne More will call you. She's a nurse, but much more than a nurse. She can help you."

When the call did not come, I called the hospital where Ellen had received radiation therapy. From this hospital, which served as her base, Anne More worked with children who had cancer, visiting homes, trying to help parents meet the needs of their sick children.

Anne's voice was pleasant and cheerful. "I didn't want to bother you now. Most people would rather not be reminded of the illness during the holidays."

My response was wry. "We are reminded anyway. Please come."

Anne came, crisp and efficient in her white uniform, carefully casual in her first contact with us. She wondered how Ellen felt she could be of help.

Ellen responded. "Can you help us find a heated swimming pool where I could swim this winter?" She was still fighting her battle for freedom of movement.

10

The year was at an end. Conflicting feelings of deep intensity rocked each one of us. For myself, I realized, as I looked back on the autumn just past, that each holiday celebrated since that October conference had carried a feeling of finality. Each was tagged in my mind as the last of its kind that Ellen would see. Ellen's sixteenth birthday in November had been especially poignant—a stark contrast to the folk-music celebration of the previous year, the last birthday of pre-cancer-diagnosis days.

There were times when individually and collectively we all experienced feelings of being caught in a giant trap: Ellen would never get well and she would never die. Our present life would go on forever. None of us would ever again be able to live our own lives free from the tyranny of the illness. Sometimes the burden seemed unbearable. Jana and I talked about this—for clearly Ellen's numbered days had already stretched beyond her doctor's expectations.

With the Christmas holidays upon us Jana took a much needed respite from our home. She went, with Tim and Cary, to Berkeley where for a brief time she could again be her own person.

She would return. She was committed. There was no way for any of us to take our freedom now. Our task lay in helping to see Ellen through.

VI

1972: WINTER AND EARLY SPRING
Pain

Like a train pounding down some track
Throbbing, throbbing . . .
Hitting hard, Oh so fast
Straight head on, Knock down path.

Sore bent body, stiff troubled limbs
Tired, Oh God, more than tired
Spirit rung out, empty, and dry
That's what pain leaves you . . .
*   And if it's not a death wish*
*   It's as close as you'll come.*

Ellen, *March, 1972*

1

Novato, Calif.
January 7, 1972

*D*ear Beth,
    You seemed interested in the making of the candle—so here goes.
    At first I couldn't figure out how it was made either, until a
friend of my sister's did it for me. First of all, what you see as the
top of the candle is actually the bottom. It's made upside down. The

mold has a small hole in it at the bottom where the wick goes through and is bent flat. Then the mold is tilted at certain angles to get the required effects that are wanted as the layers of different colors are poured on one by one, and each layer is left to harden somewhat one by one. Then it is taken out of that mold and maybe placed in another of the same size except this one has upside down trees carved in its sides. When hot wax is poured down over the sides, the tree shapes are filled in. That's one possible way to do the trees, but they could have been painted on by hand. Or cellophane could have been wrapped around the candle to get that effect. Well, that was hell to think all through and write down—I'll say!

In your candle I saw a landscape of a swampy marshland just at dusk. I can picture the fog rolling in through the trees and the tule mist rising up from the bog and the river.

I've been wanting to find a place to swim—it's a way I can use my muscles and body, just about the only way. I can't run or anything, so swimming is a good thing. Well, we've found it. A nurse I know found out about it. A woman who once herself had breast cancer and went through all the surgery and radiation treatment, recovered—had the pool built so she could begin to use those muscles again. It's been five years since the cancer for her now, and she hasn't wanted the pool to go to waste. All her children have grown, and I guess she doesn't use it too much herself. She is really a very fine person who has gone through a lot of hard times and I like her very much. I went swimming today, and I'd forgotten how much it wears you out.

Elaine is the woman with this pool, and she said something that made me feel really good. She said—"You know it's at times like this that it's time to get out and live. If you lay in bed all the time wondering if you're going to live or die or when—then you're dead already." And I feel it's true, if you just lay in bed all the time, crying and sad, then you are as good as dead, whether you're sick or not. Because you're not being alive, you're not feeling alive.

*Beth, I want to tell you thank you for your words—I hear them
very clear.*

Love you,
El

*Also for me school is very good this year. With just the two
periods, I have the time to really fully (try to) understand the
knowledge that is being shoved at me.*

*Be prepared for a late Channuka present. It was made by
Troy, my very good friend. If you look close in the lower right hand
corner I think you'll see the signature. Next time you write tell me
what you see in it.*

Love again,
El

2

During that winter Ellen became engulfed by pain. At
first there were bad days or nights and good days or nights.
The pain would recede after hours of pounding at her. It
seemed to be connected with swelling of her leg and foot.
We watched carefully. Dr. Lorin cautioned now after each
treatment that swelling and pain would result. He asked
Ellen to rest, and she spent much time lying on the sofa
with her leg elevated. She remained quite tolerant of the
pain as long as she associated it with fighting the illness.
When the pain hit, the combinations of medicines, which
Dr. Alton and Dr. Kramer had worked out together, were
no longer effective in small doses. Anne, the nurse who had
begun visiting us in December, watched this development
as it took place. She alerted Dr. Kramer. He prescribed
larger and larger dosages of the pills, trying to get on top of
the pain.

On good days, Ellen still went to school—trying to maintain her relationships with her friends. She feared losing touch with Lurene and Judy. She fought to maintain her contact with them, but it was a losing battle. Her friendship with Troy continued. They listened to music together, and occasionally Ellen went to Free Youth meetings with him.

She went on fighting for freedom of movement: she and Jana took trips to the ocean, and sometimes we went to the heated pool which Anne had found for us.

Treatment with Dr. Lorin and consultations with Dr. Kramer continued; Ellen and Jana tried to see Frances each week; and Anne came, stopping in at pre-arranged times, carefully observing and storing up data about Ellen's situation. She made concrete suggestions about ways to deal with the swelling. She asked few questions, but was clearly interested in helping Ellen to manage the pain, whether physical or emotional.

At first Ellen saw no need to talk to yet another person. But as Anne remained available for listening, while immensely practical and knowledgeable about increasing her comfort, Ellen opened up. There were times now when she felt too ill to keep her appointments with Frances, and gradually she found herself sharing her feelings and problems with Anne. It was thus that Anne moved into our life—skilled nurse becoming trusted friend, rendering manageable that which seemed unmanageable.

3

Winter continued. The swelling and throbbing pain came more often, no longer clearly associated with the treatment. It was obvious that walking, even with crutches, now caused severe swelling. Reluctantly, sadly, it was conceded that the tumor was larger now and was pressing on a major vein, interfering with the return of blood from Ellen's leg. Edema, swelling, and severe throbbing pain were the results.

Days became bad. School, friendships, pleasures and distractions could not be enjoyed. Ellen lay on the sofa, her leg and foot raised on cushions, seeking help from the force of gravity in coaxing the swelling down from her foot.

The days were bad, but the nights were worse. Drowsy with fatigue and medication, but awakened by her bladder's decreased ability to store fluid, Ellen stumbled to the bathroom during the night, trying to take care of her own body functions, trying not to awaken the family. But during many of these night trips, she experienced severe bladder spasms. We would wake to her cry, and I could only go in to hold her, weeping in sympathy with her pain.

We returned to the urologist and his younger associate. They were both enormously compassionate, giving of their time and energy. They established control over the spasms by varying the medicines, and were always available and helpful in using their skill to make Ellen more comfortable. Contact with them continued over many months, through several urinary tract infections and other emergencies.

Severe as this difficulty was, it became more bearable through talking with these doctors and learning of some options. Because of frequent night trips to the bathroom, Ellen's rest was disturbed. The doctors explained about bladder catheters and urine collection bags—no surgery would be required, the method would be simple to initiate and maintain, and could be removed if the situation changed.

Ellen considered the possibility and decided against it. She had too much to do; she didn't want a catheter and bag getting in her way. The doctors listened and accepted her refusal. They went on trying to help her deal with difficulties as they arose.

4

In February, having steeled herself for painful answers, Ellen asked her questions of Dr. Kramer.

"Is the tumor growing?"

"Yes."

"How long will I live?"

"Six months to two years."

It was a silent trip home that late afternoon; we had acknowledged that the illness would win. What lay ahead now was an attempt to focus on the quality of the time that remained.

In March, Dr. Kramer suggested that Ellen put aside the crutches for her outside activities and use a wheelchair instead. He pointed out that this would put less strain on her body and actually make it possible for her to be more active outside of the house. With the beginning of this second spring of her illness, it seemed important that Ellen be taken to places which she could enjoy. The emphasis now was on 'taken.' To Ellen, it seemed that—with the wheelchair—her personal freedom of movement would be totally gone.

David brought home a wheelchair—shiny metal and cheerful blue fabric, lightweight, easily folded and transportable. Ellen wept.

5

Dr. Lorin was in conflict. He was confident that with the transfer factor and BCG he could keep the lung metastasis down to the same minimal spot. X-rays supported his belief. It was important to his research to find out how long this process could be maintained. He believed that in carrying on his research he was also prolonging Ellen's life. But he witnessed Ellen's increasing pain and disability. He knew that death from the pelvic sarcoma, choking off the function of internal organs, would probably be far more painful than death from lung cancer. He wondered about continuing with the transfer factor.

During that period from late winter through early spring, there were several long talks between Ellen and Dr. Lorin. We came to his new lab, a huge barn-like structure, which was being set up in the city. We came after working hours when technicians and other workers were gone; only Dr. Lorin and his dog waited for us, shot ready, concern and friendship also present.

With pride, he showed us the new equipment being purchased by the hospital. He talked of plans for computerized processes which would diagnose cancer before it became the terrible life-devouring monster it now was.

We also talked about Ellen—her friends, her activities, her feelings. It was clear to us as we talked, that choices did still remain. Discouraged and in pain, Ellen questioned going on with treatment, or indeed going on with living. An alternative did exist: that of stopping, of getting off, of curling up and dying. There were ways of using the pain medication so that her way out would be eased. Ellen reserved the right to do this if she wished, knowing that I would support and help her.

She came back to the other alternative—that of going on and using her days to the fullest. With this option came the continuation of treatment. She made the choice, and she lived it with all the grace she could muster.

6

In spite of control over urinary difficulties, the pain in Ellen's entire right side was becoming intense, excruciating at times. In desperation after a particularly bad night, I called Anne one early morning in March.

"What are we going to do about the pain, Anne? We can't go on."

Anne, practical, unperturbable, gentle yet supportive, moved quickly and decisively. She arranged an evening conference with Dr. Kramer. We met her and went together to the doctor's office. Here we talked at length about alternatives in dealing with the pain. We explored the usefulness and effectiveness of pills as compared to shots. David explained his misgivings about shots: the problem of going to stronger and stronger drugs, each in turn becoming less effective as the body adapted to it.

Ellen was strongly influenced by her father. She was set against drugs in general and hated shots of any kind. Yet she was trying to deal with pain which she could no longer handle—not by large doses of pills, not by self-hypnosis or meditation, nor by loving support from doctors, family, and friends.

Anne dealt with Ellen's objections. "You need the relief from pain. You can't enjoy anything as things are. You need sleep and rest now. We'll deal with other problems if and when they come up."

Jana offered to give the shots. Ellen listened and was persuaded. David conceded. Dr. Kramer prescribed strong pain killers and needles and, during the next few days, Anne taught us how to give shots. We practiced with needles and water on oranges: fill, measure, spurt, needle into orange, aspirate, send fluid in, withdraw needle. Using the needle to pierce the orange was easy. Using it to quickly and surely pierce Ellen's skin and send the narcotic into her muscle was something else. It did not become easy.

7

The shift continued: crutches to wheelchair, oral medication to shots, classes at school to home teaching. In March her teachers and the high school worked out a flexible program—the teachers coming to Ellen's home after school hours on days when she had not appeared at school. They recognized and honored her wish to come to school whenever possible.

A shift in friendships occurred: Lurene, her friend of junior high and high school days was gone. For her the contact with the illness was unbearable. She could not deny it, and she could not rise above it. But other friends moved in, some of whom had been early childhood friends and now were renewing contact.

There was a shift, long-delayed but inevitable, in the relationship with Troy. The turning point occurred one Sunday after what had been a pain-wracked night. He came to visit, riding his bike the three-mile distance from his home. Jana was gone for the weekend. David and I were undisguisedly pleased to see him, glad for a change of focus from endurance to pleasure. Ellen rallied from a sad dream-like reverie and they listened to records, talking a little about casual things. It was no longer possible to talk about the illness in terms of conquering, in terms of strength of will or mind.

All pretense of politeness put aside, David and I slept that afternoon, overcome by exhaustion from the previous night's battle against the pain. As the two young people talked, Ellen too drifted off into sleep, lying back in her big leather-like reclining chair. And Troy was left—the only person awake in that house—as the plaintive flute notes of a favorite song continued to come from the record player.

For a long time Troy sat, silent and alone. That day, he knew he had lost Ellen to the illness. He felt that he was powerless to ease her pain. Right now he could not even reach her to share this moment of temporary relief from the pain. He would have to go on his own way.

Perhaps he himself was not aware of the decisiveness of that day. But when he arose, turned off the record player, and left the silent house, he rode his bike away and out of her life. He continued to visit, as did his parents, but for his own safety and well-being, he erected a wall of self-protection, a wall of concentration on, and utter preoccupation with, his music and art. He shifted from high school to junior college courses, and expended his energy in the heavy labor of house-painting and other paid jobs. Ellen felt the change. It was very hard for her to relinquish the relationship, but in this there was no option.

8

Our task was hard. We met it by total sharing. It was a dogged day-by-day, night-by-night battle. Our enemy was pain. Shots became a part of Ellen's life. Oral medication continued and the shots were used mainly in the late afternoon, when pain had become intolerable, or at night to purchase some sleep and comfort. Ellen regarded the shots as defeat, pointing up what she saw as her inability to take the pain. But we pulled together in reassuring her. While Jana or I gave the shot, David held Ellen. Then he would sit with her, talking softly or reading in a monotone until the medicine took over. We tried to keep ahead of the pain, anticipating rather than following up with the medicine. But by April it was not possible to provide more than short two-hour periods of time which were relatively free from pain.

Tim and Cary had left, by request, and found other housing. In this home, there was no longer time or room for debates on whose turn it was to do household jobs or chores. Supported by Anne, Ellen had been able to make clear her present need for absence of commotion. The large jointly-prepared communal dinners no longer provided her with pleasure or distraction. So, despite our misgivings that Jana would also leave, David and I had honored Ellen's needs and asked the young men to leave.

Jana stayed. "I said I'd stay through the school year. And I will."

By the time April came, I was ready to relinquish Ellen. The child I had known was gone; her innocence, enthusiasm and exploration cut short by the pain which wracked her body. I knew in my own mind that I would have used the shots at any time to help Ellen leave, had she been ready to go.

But she was not ready to go, and we held on, fighting the crashing waves of pain, seeking whatever small islands of relief and comfort were still possible.

9

This was a time of much private thinking for Ellen. There were times of comparative peace and tranquility between onslaughts of pain. She wrote poetry. Letters from or to her friends, written as she lay back in her enveloping, supporting chair, became her chief pleasure. Her letters spoke of her reality. Her poems spoke of her pain, her wishes, her longing. On rare occasions she played her flute. But, most of the time, the melodies of recorded music which she loved and shared with Jana became an ever-present background when she was awake, and sometimes even while she slept.

In mid-April, she received a letter from a young man whom she had never met. He was a young black man, caught in California's prison system. For a time he was at a vocational training institution in Northern California. While there, he learned about Ellen from a friend of Jana's, who was interested in prison reform and prisoner visitation programs.

Tracy, Calif.
April 16, 1972

Dear Ellen,

I received a letter from Carol Friday and she gave me your address as someone wanting to communicate with a captive. She also told me a little about you. Of course she told me about your having cancer which touched me rather deeply. I'm very interested in communicating and exchanging ideas and warmth with you. My life is committed to people. I'm dedicated to pulling the heart out of the capitalistic monster and drowning its tentacles in the sea of People's rage—People's war. Therefore I find myself bound to you as a part of the masses, more importantly as a human. So feel free to

*call on me as a soldier who's ears are receptive to the beat of another
comrade.*

Carol told me you really had some good criticism of the
Dialectics of Sex. *I also read the book and I'd like to hear your
comments.*

*I'd hope that we both could inject a little bit of spirit into one
another, because I personally am becoming very discouraged. People
outside do give lip service to supporting the captives within the
dungeons of hell. But the manner in which they express their
comradeship is based on some jive, phony, bourgeois idea, rather
than solidarity and positive struggle. I guess I sound bitter, that's
right—four-hundred-and-fifty-years worth. Still, politics guide my
thinking as well as my actions. I hope these few words carry with
them warmth and sincerity. I remain open and receptive to you.*

Strong in Chains

Barron

P.S. Answer soon

Ellen did not answer him then. She put her thoughts
and feelings into her poetry.

Spring, 1972

Controller
A sharp poison, you are that
If this much I dwell upon you
A whole part of my life you've become.
I look back with surprise in my head.

Waiting Out Death
This constant pressing flow of pain
My life has come to be.
Is it worth what strength I've left
To fight on constantly.

Ellen

Spring, 1972

On Being White

*I know your ancestors went through
much pain and sorrow.*

> *I know as much as I was told.
> I see you too have many hardships.
> Am I as guilty as I feel?*

*I call you brother in this human
race. Will you never acknowledge to me
the same?*

> *Whitey! Honky! Cracker!
> I am the recipient of your anger.
> These words when meant for me, I hurt.
> Please don't judge me by my color.*

I am ignorant of your troubles. I imagine, while watching film strips in my school about ghettos and misconceptions between your color and mine—Troubles, hard times I can't even touch, I can't feel it. Like I said, I only imagine and watch film strips too. So I say how very sorry I am. But it is very late and it does no good.

Ellen

April, 1972

*Give me spring days—shining
Where lupins, clover, and dandelion weeds
Row on from field to field.
Give me green grasses, tips full of dew.*

*Well the day travels on as I lay in the field
Soaking up warmth in my sleep.
Later I turn on my back, watching the sky
Through petals of a flower I hold to my eye.*

Sudden realization that the sun has moved on
Five places west while I rested on.
Mist rolls up over the hills all around
Down it creeps low upon the sleeping town.

Ellen

Ellen saw and talked with Frances, no longer on a weekly schedule, but when her body could tolerate the car ride into San Francisco. They talked now about giving up. They explored Ellen's fears and hopes. They believed and accepted our promise that Ellen would never be put into a hospital—that whatever came, we would see it through together at home.

With Frances, Ellen was able to go on past fear to thoughts of her own death.

10

Through that winter of pain, Jana carried the days with courage and without complaint. She could not be all that she wished to be. No one could. Her wishes even infiltrated her sleep during those mid-April nights. Many days later, she told me about one dream.

"I had a dream about Ellen. I dreamed that we were both sitting in the living room—she, in her chair, me, on the floor by her. A song called 'Matty Groves' by the Fairport Convention was on the record player. It has a good beat, and in my dream I started to dance. Then I looked down and realized that Ellen was very light. I picked her up in my arms—in the dream she didn't weigh anything at all—so we danced like that for a long time. I felt so free!"

And Jana's friend Karen-lee, who had shared our home on many occasions, wrote to Ellen from North Carolina.

Raleigh, North Carolina
April 23, 1972

Dearest Ellen,
Hope this finds you strong. I have thought of you so many times. Your love has helped me in so many ways. Please be strong and remember that I love you.

Your friend for eternity,
Karen-lee

VII

1972: LATE SPRING
Renewal

Do not believe that
he who seeks to
comfort you lives
untroubled among the
simple and quiet words
that sometimes do you good.

His life has much
difficulty and
sadness and
remains far behind
yours.

Were it otherwise he
would never have
been able to find
these words.

R. M. Rilke
to Ellen from Anne
May 5, 1972

1

By mid-April, it had become clear that this pain was intractable. With Dr. Kramer and Anne, David and I faced our options. One alternative was hospitalization for relief through narcotics given intravenously. This meant that Ellen would be hospitalized indefinitely, kept in bed by intravenous tubes, dependent upon hospital personnel for help in her body functions. We refused this.

"We can't do that to her. We promised."

Through persistent efforts by Dr. Lorin's young medical assistant, Dr. Kramer had become aware of another option. He now presented this option to us: it was neurosurgery —cutting the spinal cord in just the right place to interrupt the messages of pain that flashed between that lower right side and her spinal cord and brain. It would require an extremely gifted neurosurgeon. Dr. Kramer would explore the possibilities at the university hospital.

Two days later he called back, guardedly optimistic. He thought he had interested a highly skilled surgeon. I was to call Dr. Pennington for an appointment.

Bluntly Dr. Kramer told me, "He said he wouldn't touch it unless the patient has four months."

I held my breath, "What did you say?"

"I said yes."

Quick, to the point, ever-practical, no-nonsense Kramer. He considered the alleviation of pain his primary responsibility with Ellen. He moved to defeat it.

Before calling for an appointment, we talked with Ellen and Jana, examining our choices. If we reached a decision in favor of the operation, it would mean hospitalization. But hospitalization, not just to suffer and die. It would be temporary hospitalization to deal with the specific problem of unbearable pain. Ellen considered and then said that she didn't know, couldn't know, until she had seen the surgeon. The options and alternatives were now few. But she wanted them kept open.

I called the surgeon's office and in his busy schedule the secretary found an appointment several weeks away. I said simply, "That isn't possible. We can't wait that long."

After brief consultation on the other end of the line, the message was, "He'll stay late in his office to see you next Tuesday. Can you come at five o'clock?"

"Yes."

2

We went to the office. The wheelchair was now our constant companion, Ellen's self-consciousness put aside by her inability to walk without intense pain.

Dr. Pennington examined Ellen and talked with her. Then, while the nurse helped her, he began to talk with David and me. Ellen was annoyed at being excluded from any information-sharing or decision-making and made her feelings clear to the nurse. So David, who knew Ellen must share in the total process, wheeled her into the office.

Interrupted by several phone calls from doctors seeking his advice, Dr. Pennington was brusque and impatient, authoritative in his responses to his callers. His manner of dealing with these interruptions was in counterpoint to the gentleness and completeness with which he talked to us: yes, he could see how painful Ellen's situation was, and yes, he thought he could help. He explained the method of surgery, the location of the planned incision, and the hoped-for result. He went into some detail about the problems involved, but was optimistic that he could obtain desirable results. There was always the chance of greater involvement, of impairment of function or movement in the entire lower half of Ellen's body. But he hoped to limit the surgical effect to the lower right quadrant of her body. This side would become numb. She would not get sensations of heat, cold, or fatigue—but she would also not get sensations of pain. There would be some loss of free movement of this side, but right now her total movement was severely curtailed by her pain.

Knowing the dangers and limitations, Ellen chose to have the surgery. The doctor offered her a choice of hospitals: he would bring his own surgical team and he wanted Ellen to pick the hospital which she thought would be most comfortable for her.

She made her choice and there was no talk of delay or busy schedules. He scheduled Ellen's surgery for the beginning of the following week.

During the intervening days, Ellen wrote to Beth and Charlene, her letters matter-of-fact, a unique blend of trivia and statement of life-altering developments.

Novato, Calif.
April 27, 1972

Hi Beth,

Just got done washing my hair. It feels really good—like when you splash yourself with the hose on a super-hot day.

Got a wheelchair now. At first the whole idea of sitting in one put my mind in a bad place.

But I figure the days are getting more and more beautiful. I would want to go walking through parks and just be out in the sunshine a whole lot. So, I'll sacrifice my vanity and sit in the damn thing.

I'm just thinking back to my visit to Oak Park with you. I remember all the record stores we went to, and I remember Evanston. I liked it there especially.

I have home-teaching now. Spanish II and Black Literature. I'm a lot happier learning this way—at home. I don't think I'll ever go back to High School because through the one-to-one contact you get with the person who is teaching you, you learn so much more and are able to go at your own pace.

I'm doing a lot more writing—like poetry type things. It's calming in a way that is different than anything else. It's like letting your insides free; anything you have that is bothering your mind can come out.

Been reading Seize the Time *by Bobby Seale. It tells about his life and the forming of the Black Panther Party. It's really good. He writes it as if he were reliving it.*

A person my sister knows—well, she told him about me. And he wanted to know if I felt isolated in any way, and she said, "Yeah she feels lonely." He said he'd like to come and read with me and keep me company. His name is Rick. Our first meeting was really nice. There was no surface-type talk, we just kind of dug in and got to know each other. He says he has felt isolated many times himself and so, he thought perhaps he could give me company. And he does very much. He's very open—talkative. Sometimes he talks over my head, but I let him know and make sure he re-explains.

I feel kind of like the world is closing up to me. But I won't think that—it's not so. The world has always been open to everyone. It must be the person's choice to take hold of it. It's there. It's your choice of whether you want to live or not.

A woman I know is in an organization called Connections. It helps get prisoners more in contact with the world by helping to get their relatives to them, by becoming personal friends with them and helping to educate them on what is happening in the world and in the prison movement. It is individuals working with other isolated individuals. Carol, the woman I was talking about—asked if I wanted to write letters with a captive. So she gave my address to someone she knew. I got his first letter a few days ago and it was very warm. He, Barron Bradwell, is very into the prison movement.

I suppose you know about the surgery by now. I am afraid. But still I will face it—because I can't stand this pain anymore. It sure is hell to live with.

I pray I have good luck.

All my love,
Ellie-O

Novato, California
April 30, 1972

Dear Charlene,

I'm going into the hospital tomorrow, May 1. The pain I've been in has gotten to the point of not being able to be dealt with by any type of medication—oral or shots. So they are going to operate by cutting the feeling nerves that go to my leg. That means a numb right leg. It's either that or a life of this hellish pain I've been experiencing the past three months. My choice is obvious.

"Up the Down Stair-Case" a movie that's on television is driving me nutty while I'm trying to write this letter to you.

I'll write soon again after I'm recuperated.

Love,
El

3

Jana and I took Ellen to the hospital in San Francisco. It was not the university hospital, which by now Ellen hated. It was a large, long-established hospital devoted primarily to helping children with severe illness or disability. It was near Dr. Kramer's office and he was on its staff.

Ellen was established in a large comfortable room overlooking a busy thoroughfare. The nurses and technicians, apparently versed in ways of putting young people at ease, took over. Ellen watched them, amused. David joined us, and the evening passed with some feeling of anticipation rather than dread. The food was good and Ellen seemed comfortable. David, Jana and I left, after stopping at the desk to make sure the staff understood Ellen's need for heavy pain-medication during the night. They assured us that Dr. Kramer had left orders for Ellen to have pain-relief pills and shots "on demand." Reassured, we went home, David and I planning to return early enough the following morning to see Ellen before she was taken to surgery.

When we returned, however, we found that Ellen had been taken from her room earlier than planned, and another long wait began.

4

Hours later, Ellen emerged from the shadow of the anesthesia, relieved of her heavy burden of pain. There were elements of comedy and irony in that day. The previous night, after we had gone and the nursing staff shift had changed, Ellen's pain, intensified by her anxiety, had become unbearable. The nurse in charge, feeling perhaps that there was some error in the order, refused to provide heavy narcotics "on demand." Conscientiously, she had provided pain-relief medication every four hours during the night, but that didn't begin to touch Ellen's agony. After a very hard night, Ellen had been wheeled into surgery.

Now, after surgery—with family, friends, and doctors around her—she experienced utter euphoria at the relief from pain. Dr. Pennington, triumph and delight showing through the cool professional exterior, checked out the sensations in Ellen's right side, and affirmed his success in blocking out pain with a minimum of incapacitation. As he left, I walked down the corridor with him. I wondered whether there might be a drug withdrawal problem now that the pain had been eliminated. He, enormously pleased with the task he had accomplished, assured me that Dr. Kramer would handle it.

Dr. Kramer was chagrined that his order of the previous night had been disregarded. He renewed the order, making clear his displeasure. And so the nurses found themselves in the unfamiliar position of offering shots and pills to Ellen who was still angry about the previous night. She refused the medicines. She found the post-operative pain and discomfort so much milder than the pounding agony of the past four months, that she refused all but the mildest oral medication.

The nurses began to be concerned that she would have withdrawal symptoms with the sudden stopping of the narcotics—but Dr. Kramer, when contacted, supported Ellen in allowing her the dignity of judging for herself what she needed.

During those days of hospitalization following the operation, Ellen chose abrupt and complete cessation of habituating pain-relief drugs. She found support and comfort in our continual presence—Jana and I took turns staying with her during the days, and David again dozed through the nights in a chair pulled up beside her bed. She experienced no symptoms of withdrawal, except for some intestinal disturbance which might or might not have been related. Her doctors were elated. The successful surgery combined with blood transfusions and good medical management provided Ellen with a feeling of enormous wellbeing. It seemed to her that she had been born again.

She could no longer lift her right foot and knee in walking; she needed the help of a walking-aid—but this was a price that had been foreseen. She left the hospital, thin and frail, but with good appetite and color, feeling respected, aware of her own contribution to the accomplishment of that week.

Dr. Kramer and Anne cautioned us that swelling of Ellen's right leg and foot would still be a problem. A new problem—that of numbness on the right side—could cause trouble. We barely heard this second caution, so thankful were we for the cessation of pain.

Life was again worth living. Ellen experienced the month of May as a peak of relief and with the sheer enjoyment of being. Limitations of movement were regretted but accepted. Friendships and relationships took on new intensity and meaning with the haze of pain and heavy medication removed. Ellen looked outward again. Her zest to continue living led to a renewal of interest in the transfer factor and BCG therapy. We made plans to see Dr. Lorin during the first week in June.

5

Confident now that she could leave Ellen for awhile, Jana began to make plans for a trip to see her friend Karenlee in North Carolina. Ellen seemed quite willing for Jana to go.

During this time a letter came from Chris, the friend of Ellen's early childhood horse-and-rider play-fantasy days.

Oakton, Virginia
May 30, 1972

Dear Ellen,

We received a letter from Mrs. Strauss today and in it she told us that she had talked with your mother and she told her what has been happening. I don't know what to say, Ellen. All this time I have wondered why you hadn't written, I am so sorry. I'm trying to find the right words, but I can't. All I can say is that I am praying for your recovery, praying very hard.

You know, I am leaving for Los Angeles a week from this Friday, on the 9th of June. I am going back to visit all my friends in Thousand Oaks. I am seriously thinking of maybe taking a bus up to see you. Now all I have to do is ask Mom and Dad. They are on vacation now and I am staying at some friend's house. I am going to try very hard to convince them.

Not much has been going on. Here we are in Virginia, our eleventh move. Help! I am finally getting used to it. I would rather live in California, but then again, who wouldn't?

I guess there isn't much else to say. Please do send me your phone number; it means a lot to me. I hope you are doing better and I send you God's blessings and all my love. I love you!

Chris

6

May, 1972

Today was a very beautiful day. In the morning the sky was cloudy, but the sun later broke through the clouds and it shone down on the land. I slept on the lawn while the sun warmed me. The fragrance of the flowers was all around me. In the evening the sky was gold in color with clouds of blue. I watched the sun that slipped off behind the mountains.

Ellen

May, 1972

I reach toward the heaven
To soar like an eagle,
Free in the wild winds
To live as I will.

I dream that I'm flowing
On legs of a swift horse,
Through the deep canyons.
I live as I will.

My mind goes on racing
As fast as my heart beats.
I think back on times
That are special to me.

Now I hope for the future
And pray that it's coming.
Somehow I hold to
"There must be a way!"

It's somehow ironic—
My fate is my fortune.
I've learned much in life now,
Think sometimes too much.

Ellen

May, 1972

Intensely they live
each hour of the day
In purposeful waiting
and purposeful flight . . . .

They burst into song
    or soar with the winds
A deep sense of urgency
    prevails through their lives.

They have their limitations—as all things do
Yet they live so fully within their sphere, that birds
Shall ever seem to be . . . .
        wild . . . .
            beautiful . . . .
                and free . . . .
                        Ellen

Young babes are born
and grow then to old folks.

And from this growing
there comes much change.

So in their changing
people will see true.

And with this sight
they shall be young.
                        Ellen

VIII

1972: SUMMER
Choices

*I wake at dawn
with a winged heart
and give thanks for
another day of loving.*

Kahil Gibran

1

Ellen wrote to friends, and received their letters.

*Tracy, California
June 5, 1972*

Dear El,
    I received your very moving letters today and you pierce the depths of my mind. Unveiling and beckoning unto me a very human experience. Which makes me want to become a part of your experience in some meaningful way.
    I feel a relief myself just hearing you aren't burdened with so much pain. I'm glad you're reading and doing some of the things which bring meaning to you.
    Your poem made me sad, but it also reminded me that I'm a fighter. Your verses had a very relaxed and sensitive flow. We have

a lot in common—first and foremost we're two people trying to sincerely express that affection and concerned feeling human beings try to give to one another. You too are a fighter.

Your response to the captives was very enlightening. You touched on some very positive points, which describe our conditions and just how people relate to us. I guess it's pretty hard for people to feel a real closeness to us. Which means we're going to have to try and educate people to our needs and why it's so important that they have a real interest in our conditions. People out there need to get involved with the captives on every level possible, visiting, visiting, etc. Good intentions will no longer serve to bridge the gap.

Tell me more about your family. And just anything you want me to know about you. Feel free to ask about me or anything you may want to ask or confide in me. My effort will be true and always in consideration of you.

Don't give up on life. We're both fighters fighting together.

> *In revolutionary love,*
> *Barron*

P.S. I'm awaiting your picture. When I get a chance I'll send you one.

> *Laurel, Mississippi*
> *June 8, 1972*

Dearest Ellen,

I just got off the phone from talking to you. You sounded just great. And you have really helped me. I was so depressed. I don't know why.

I'm glad that you and Jana were home. By the way, how far is North Carolina from Mississippi? I had no idea. Jan asked me.

> *I love you guys,*
> *Charlene*

P.S. See you some day, I hope.

2

Jana and Ellen were planning a party. Invitations went out to many friends. There was much to celebrate. It was early June, school was ending. Ellen would be completing her work with the home teachers, I would be finished with the school year—an accomplishment made possible only by the cooperation of the entire family. Jana would be released. She had kept her promise, more than her promise, and would be free to explore her own life, to travel, perhaps to see her friend Karen-lee in North Carolina.

But the exultant note in the celebration was surely not one of completion of tasks; it was one of conquest of pain. Since the operation, Ellen's recuperation at home had been steady and sure. At home she no longer used crutches. She walked with the help of a walking aid—a sturdy metal frame which she placed in front of her with each step. On trips out of the house, the wheelchair was put in the back seat or trunk of the car. But much of the time it went unused.

Days before the party, Ellen and I had seen first Dr. Kramer and then Dr. Lorin. With Dr. Kramer, it was time to say goodbye. Dr. Alton had returned from Europe and would soon be back in his office, resuming his practice. It was time for me to call that office and make arrangements for transferring Ellen's care.

The farewell to Dr. Kramer was emotional. We had been through much together—we had all learned from the experience. It seemed to me that Ellen was now in better condition, physically and emotionally, than she had been in many months. And I was grateful.

We went then to Dr. Lorin's lab—another triumphal stop. He gave Ellen a shot of transfer factor. He cautioned us about lymphocytic reaction and possible swelling. He advised rest and elevation of the now-numb leg. But in our exhilaration we hardly heard the caution and it went unheeded.

So with work well-done and pain controlled, the summer stretched ahead: a golden time, a time of conscious choice of experiences, pleasures and relationships which would be meaningful to Ellen. So well did Ellen feel that, in her conversations, she again gave the impression of believing that she had a lifetime ahead of her—one of physical limitations to be sure, but one unencumbered by pain and not menaced by imminent death, or a wish for it.

3

And so the party: it was given in our house on a Friday evening in mid-June. The rooms were filled with people —young friends of Ellen and Jana, and adults who had remained in our life or moved into it with friendship and support as the illness had progressed. Troy was there. He played his guitar.

Dressed in a long, flowing, colorful dress which covered her disabled leg, seated on the raised hearth of the fireplace, Ellen talked with Troy, listened to the music, and glowed. Her facial expression and coloring, enhanced by the blood transfusions of several weeks ago, told of life and determination, not of death or resignation.

She sat with her legs down, like anyone else, moving about very little, but pleased at being part of this large group of people, laughing and talking, listening to music, enjoying life.

4

That was Friday night. By Sunday morning Ellen was in extreme pain—not in her numb right leg, but in her left pelvic area with pain shooting down her left side. She was dismayed and frightened. Her right leg was swollen, but this she had expected as a price for the activity so soon after the shot of transfer factor. She had planned to rest and elevate her leg during the rest of the weekend following the party. She had not expected the pain.

We were disheartened. David called Dr. Alton. Days earlier, I had called Dr. Alton's office, jubilant that Ellen was still here to resume her relationship with him. An appointment had been made for the following week, since Ellen was feeling well and there was no emergency.

Now we could not delay. We met in the quiet Sunday-morning emptiness of Dr. Alton's office. He moved back into Ellen's life on the tide of this emergency. He came strengthened and deepened by the time spent in study and observation abroad. With gentle sureness, he examined Ellen. He talked with her; he talked with David and me. He believed that this present pain was possibly caused by the transfer factor as it created lymphocytic activity around the tumor. Swelling then created pressure on nerves, and pain messages were relayed all through the lower half of her body. The lower right side did not hear the messages. The lower left side now did.

That Sunday morning the doctor began his re-evaluation of Ellen's situation. He prescribed pills for the pain; medicine, new to Ellen, which would dull the pain without depressing her mood. He reached into the arsenal of chemotherapeutic agents and prescribed a drug which was often used in combination with others to suppress the body's own immune response and take over the job of killing cancer cells. These had been avoided with Ellen up to now because of the decision to follow Dr. Lorin's treatment. Now, however, it was necessary to counteract the transfer factor—its action was causing the swelling and pain. He did not make a permanent decision at this time. He planned to confer with Dr. Kramer, Dr. Lorin, Anne, and Frances—to make long-range plans for Ellen's treatment. But here, now, it was necessary to deal with the pain by turning off the transfer factor.

5

The conference was held by doctors, nurse, and social worker; recommendations and directions were agreed upon. Some choices were then offered to Ellen. They recommended that treatment by transfer factor be discontinued. It had kept down the lung metastasis, but it could not conquer the large bony pelvic tumor. It was, despite the recent surgery, going to cause pain in that tumor area and the now-affected left side. They recommended, too, that the chemotherapy begun by Dr. Alton be continued since Ellen was reacting well to it. She was not experiencing noticeable hair loss, a sometime complication of the drug, and the pain was decreasing. These were the recommendations; the choices were Ellen's. She considered and agreed that they made sense. She would accept them.

One further choice was offered Ellen: that of meeting with all three doctors together at the university hospital clinic for her continuing care, so that she could know that they all remained involved in her treatment. She declined this offer, choosing instead to see Dr. Alton in the comfort and relative quiet of his own office, closer to our home.

Ellen and I began weekly trips to this office. Now, we were together in the examining room; consultations were open between the three of us. Others in that office —doctors, nurses, technicians, and clerical people—were quietly supportive and helpful. Sometimes Anne joined us, coming over from the hospital nearby. Sometimes Dr. Lorin drove up from San Francisco to see Ellen here. Then the old wry and irreverent humor flashed between them. Messages of interest and support from Dr. Kramer were relayed to Ellen. As the pain decreased, and the medicines were carefully monitored and regulated, Ellen took hold of her life again.

Chest X-rays were taken at two-week intervals. The lung metastasis, long suppressed by the transfer factor, was now bursting into activity. In early July, Dr. Alton talked with us about the new X-rays. Ellen asked to see them as well as the old X-rays of her lungs and pelvic area. He showed them to her, explaining the pictures, pointing out the areas of cancer growth.

He offered Ellen another choice. She could have radiation therapy to the spots on her lung. This would destroy cancer cells there. He did not offer a hope of eliminating the disease, only of prolonging her days by the destructive effect of radiation on some of the cancer cells. It was a numbers game. The longer the doctors could keep the cancer cell count down, the longer Ellen might live. Penalties and prices would have to be paid: discomfort and enervation from the treatment, and continued growth of the pelvic tumor—since that area had already taken the maximum X-ray dosage.

Ellen listened that hot July day in the quiet air-conditioned office and said, "I have to talk to Anne. I can't decide now."

So we called Anne at the nearby hospital and then ventured out into the airless oppressive heat. We drove to the hospital, where Anne met us; we went in to the cool dim quiet of the hospital's professional library. There we talked—and Ellen made her choice. She would not submit her body to radiation therapy again. The price was too great. She would use her days to enjoy what she could. She was bitter—toward the illness. It was unfair. She had fought so hard and it would all come to nothing. She could not win.

That hot July day Ellen grieved and acknowledged her loss. In the days to come, she would transcend her loss and invest her hope again in the *now*.

Novato, California
July 7, 1972

Dear Chris,

Beautiful sky out tonight. The weather has been super-hot the past few days. So hot the air smelled stale, but that's finally over and the sea breeze has moved in.

I'm writing to a young man in prison. I don't know what he's in for, but I don't think it's as important as communicating with him. The White Panthers had a program going, where they talked with the inmates in prisons and found people on the outside who wanted to write to them. That's how I got in contact with Barron. Barron Bradwell is his name.

When I wake up mornings, I dread the day ahead of me. Just more fighting off of the pain, sometimes I'm lonely, sometimes I'm just really sad. But the days are good. I know that I could be going through radiation, but I'm not, I'm enjoying myself. I told you I have some spots on my lung. But I'm not going to put myself through hell and depression when it means so much more to me to be

*with the people I love. To be comfortable so I can enjoy myself.
Radiation totally drains you of energy.*

*I know how much hope you have for me. But I think this
cancer has me beat. I have already been through so many treatments
of other sorts and it is still growing. What I believe in is the love of
others, and that keeps me alive today.*

*I was having some pretty hard times with my dad. He has a
very hard time facing the seriousness of my disease. As more and
more things go wrong with my body, it's more of a blow to him each
time than to me. I've begun to accept things as they go wrong. It no
longer frightens me. I've had my fill of desperation and fear.*

Sorry to end on a sour note. I love ya.

And good times to ya,

> *Love,*
> *El*

> *Clearwater, Minnesota*
> *July 16, 1972*

Dear Ellen,

*I am so glad you wrote! I am in Minnesota at my grandpar-
ents. I received your letter yesterday. I left California June 22nd,
was home a week, then we came here. Pat forwarded your letter to
here. I almost had a heart attack when I saw the letter was from
you. At first when I hadn't heard from you when I was in
Thousand Oaks, I was really scared. I kept praying that your
letter would come, but it didn't. It's times like this, El, that I wish
we had never moved. I want to be with you so much, but here I am,
stuck 3000 miles away.*

*I can tell by your letter that this cancer has opened your heart
to the world around you. I cry to think that it takes something like
this to open our eyes. Do you know that we have known each other
for over ten years? I can't believe it. It has all gone so fast—too
fast—if only I could be with you. Your letter has made us even*

closer, I feel. I miss you so much and I am afraid that by next summer when I will be able to come to California, you won't be there.

Listen to me, me afraid—Ellen—you are a strong person—strong people make it through—Even though I am so far away, my spirit and thoughts are with you—my prayers and hopes will never pull away. I want you to know this—that I love you—I always have.

Chris

P.S. Your poem is just beautiful. Oh, by the way, I haven't a picture of you. The latest one is third grade. So if you have any, please send me one.

6

With the ending of school, Jana left to live again with other young people, and I took back a greater share of Ellen's care. She was by now terribly frail, though her spirits were high.

Problems had arisen, anticipated by Dr. Kramer and Anne when they had warned about the numbness of her right side. Pressure sores, breaks in the skin over her hip bones, had appeared, caused by insufficient turning and shifting of her body positions. With Dr. Alton's and Anne's patient help, we now tackled the difficult task of trying to heal these and prevent the beginning of other such sores.

Ellen's thinness and the limitations imposed by the swelling of her leg and numbness of her right side were in sharp contrast to her energy and strong will. She was determined to continue experiencing the pleasures and relationships which she valued. Yet to help her do this, while providing the physical care which she needed, placed me on a continual treadmill, almost obliterating my own wish to share the pleasures of each day with her. Anne and I talked about this, and about my need for occasional withdrawal and relief.

And so it was that, in mid-July, Kathleen came to help. She was a nurse and Anne's good friend. She came in response to my phone call. Anne had told me about Kathleen's recent loss of her own child, and I was hesitant to impose our situation on her. Nevertheless, at Anne's suggestion, and out of our need, I called. As we talked on the telephone, Kathleen's voice came through—pleasant, cheerful and interested. She did not speak of her own pain or grief, and we arranged for her first visit.

She came, dressed in slacks and sweater, tall, darkhaired, casual in appearance, bringing with her the beginning of a rough woolen poncho she had begun to crochet for Anne. Ellen's interest was immediately aroused by the crocheting; she wanted to learn this skill. Kathleen offered to teach her. The three of us talked, sharing our interest in needlework. Seemingly, it was a casual friendly visit—no white uniform and crisp external forms of efficiency here. Ellen was immediately pleased at the prospect of regular visits with Kathleen.

So Kathleen came, and continued to come for the rest of Ellen's life. Her visits were spaced so that on alternate days she shared afternoons with Ellen. They talked, did needlework, read separately and together—while Kathleen's trained alertness and matter-of-fact manner kept Ellen comfortable. She ministered to the pressure sores and swollen leg, she monitored and provided medicines, she took Ellen on outings, and offered observations and suggestions of wisdom and common sense.

During those afternoons I left, wandering through stores or parks, performing errands—solitary excursions from which I returned renewed and again able to take up my tasks. The arrangement took the element of desperation out of that summer and made it possible for me to concentrate on trying to put an experience of pleasure or beauty into each of Ellen's days. Some days, Kathleen was that experience of beauty. None other was necessary. Some days, Kathleen and Ellen drove to one of the parks, relaxing, talking, and sharing quiet moments in the cool green shade.

Kathleen told of her own loss: a small boy, only child, lost. It had been a desperate fight, with the exact diagnosis unclear until after his death and autopsy. Then they learned he had died of a brain tumor. Kathleen shared her experience without self-pity, with clear self-knowledge and belief in the ongoingness of life. Ellen and I shared her grief without sentimentality or pity and went on to enjoy the friendship with her.

7

During that summer Jana came and went. Her visits now contained no drudgery. They were pure friendship, willingly given, precious times for both girls. Jana's planned trip to North Carolina had not worked out. Instead Karen-lee had come to California. She and Jana visited Ellen together, sharing many light moments, as well as some deep and private communications.

Troy came but he was busy, preoccupied. He had jobs: housepainting, heavy labor which he must do to earn money for the coming year at college. He oriented himself toward the future. He anesthetized his pain about the present by his music and art, by heavy work and exhaustion.

Other friends came: some were young people who had been friends in earlier, healthy years; some were new friends, pulled by the wish to share with this girl as she continued on her way. Rick, Jana's friend, came. He related to Ellen without pity, enjoying the moments of friendship, not looking into the future.

Troy's mother, Norah, and his father came. They shared a deep friendship with Ellen. They had loved her when she was well. They loved her now. Norah, a nurse, knew what lay ahead for Ellen. But, more than a nurse, she was a deeply spiritual person who knew that the quality of the journey was more important than the destination.

Other people came; good friends—they brought their loyalty and support as gifts, priceless and irreplaceable. Dr. Danby, who had helped Ellen with the self-hypnosis, continued to come. Judy's mother came, sorrowful, bringing gifts which she had knit for Ellen. They were gifts that said, 'Stay here a while longer. Stay here and wear these. Enjoy them.' Ellen was touched and treasured these, wearing them, putting their message into each day.

8

The correspondence between Ellen and Barron took on increasing importance. Both were prisoners. They shared a profound interest in people. They shared a need to identify with each other and with other human beings who were in pain. Their friendship continued to develop through their letters—until by the end of the summer, it was a major focus in her life.

Tracy, Calif.
July 28, 1972

Dear El,
I'm just sitting here in my cell sorta daydreaming about you. Hearing from you cuts through my world of intricate political

thought. You help to remove some of the cold attitude I must adopt in order to survive in a world of steel and brutal repression. It definitely eliminates the warmth a person would normally feel. You restore much of that for me.

We have been locked in our cells twenty-four hours a day, for the last four days. Supposedly there have been some racial confrontations and some people have been hurt. But that's not totally descriptive of the conditions as they exist in reality. But I'm not going to get off into that.

I wish your dream was not just a dream. I'd like very much to come by and see you. If I ever do get out, you can be sure I will come and see you. . .

I'm not going to get a chance to finish this letter like I'd really like to, because I'm getting ready to go and eat. So I'll have to get this in the mail now, so it'll go out today.

I enjoyed the pictures. I'm going to send you the only one I have which is one of Mother and me. What I'd like for you to do is, get you one made off of the one I'm sending, and then send this one back. O.K.

If you can let me hear from you sooner this time. I look forward to hearing from you. You're growing on me. I was wondering if I could send a woman whom I relate to (a close friend) to visit with you for a day and in a way a part of me would be there. Let me know if that's okay. I'm thinking of you always. Be strong and together we shall conquer. Let it be known I am one of the people who cares about you.

Love and Struggle

We are the last generation of slaves,

Barron

P.S. Write soon, El.
P.P.S. I'll write again soon.

San Quentin, Calif.
8-10-72

Hello El,

Received your letter today. You really get off into my head,
everytime I hear from you. In short, you've made a hell of an
impact upon my life.

You're probably wondering why you haven't heard from me
before now. Well I've been transferred to San Quentin. I've been
locked up here in the hole, for ten days. I got out on the 8th. I've
been accused of being responsible for racial outbreaks. I hope you
understand me enough to know that's not true.

Of course, I don't negate the extreme racism on the part of
whites. But I definitely believe in the struggle of poor and oppressed
people, throughout the world.

I go to board in October of this year. My results will not be
favorable. I've been locked up five and a half years, four of which
were spent in the Utah State Prison. They still have a hold on me,
in which to reclaim me when I get through here. My charge there
was armed robbery, five years to life. I've been back in California
for eighteen months, on a robbery charge, five years to life. I've
spent six of those eighteen months in the hole. I spent two of the four
years under the eye of electric eyes and remote control gadgets
—maximum security, just a technological hole. Add this with a
record of every type of militant charge thinkable. And even some
unthinkable according to the thought police.

Also I've been coming to jail since early age (typical of a lot of
young blacks). I'm now twenty-four. Half of those twenty-four
years have been behind bars. I'm almost a stranger to the streets; so
when I said if I ever get out—What I meant was, I'm not sure if I'll
ever get out.

Having you there is good for me. I guess my being here isn't
quite so good for you. But I am here and for you.

You know I used to wish I had a sister. Can I just claim you?
You're very beautiful and mean very much to me. I loved your
poem. You're a very thoughtful and loving young woman.

I write poetry, but I haven't learned to write about love,
warmth and beauty. I write about anger and horror. My friend
(Betty), I told you about, tells me I need to express those things
(love, warmth, beauty). She's right, it's just that my world is
virtually without those things.

I'm glad your spirits are high. That makes me very happy to
know you're feeling so good.

You guessed right. I didn't get the newsletter. What is happen-
ing with your sister Jana?
Much love and power to you my sister,

> *Love,*
> *Barron*

9

One evening that summer, while I was away, Ellen
confronted her father. For a very long time the concentration of the family had been totally on her, and she had
needed it. Now with good medical management and support by skilled professional people, she was comfortable. For
her, today existed; tomorrow was beyond grasping for.

But her concern for David and me—her anger at us for
the gulf between us—gnawed at her. She could not be at
rest while this silence between us continued to exist. It was
a silence in one area only—that of the relationship between
the two of us. But it deeply troubled Ellen.

As they sat listening to records of music they both
enjoyed, Ellen approached her father. How did he feel about
her mother? And—oh, bitter bone of contention—how
could he ever have left his family for someone else! She was

not being fair to him. She didn't try to be. It was her desperate attempt to know him and communicate deeply with him about himself as well as about herself. It was her love for me and her desperate wish to safeguard my future, though her own was beyond rescue.

David had not expected the confrontation. He had set his levels of contact with us above the deep wells of desperation and grief within himself. He had totally devoted himself to Ellen and he could not now deal with this thrust into his own private dilemma. Caught off guard, he responded with grief and despair.

Ellen's cry was, "How could you have left us?"

David responded from the depths of his being, "But I came back."

Frightened by his intensity and his dark despair about himself, Ellen retreated. She wept. While he held her in his arms, she realized that she could only deal with her own relationship to him. She could not deal with what was between David and me.

10

Yet, as Ellen saw it, she still had the task of exploring my ability to survive should David leave. We both knew that he would not leave while Ellen lived. So as we talked, the implication was clear: could I survive if I lost Ellen and then lost David too? Ellen phrased her questions in cautious, somewhat roundabout, manner.

"How are things between you and Dad?" And then, "Do you think he will stay?"

I tried to make my response clear and direct. I had been dealing in my own mind and heart with this prospect. I now knew what I expected of myself—and while I was not sure I could hold at that level, I spoke from that expectation. I knew too what Ellen needed to hear.

"I don't know what he will do, Ellen. But I do know that whatever he does, I will be all right."

And Ellen seemed satisfied. It was as much as life could promise her. She wanted to believe me.

Weeks later, however, during one of our outings, a picnic shared with Frances, she returned to this painful topic. We were sitting on the grass beside a small lake in one of San Francisco's parks. Geese ventured close by. With delight, held over from her childhood days, Ellen threw bread to them, talking to them, admonishing the greedy, encouraging the reticent.

As Frances sat with us, Ellen told me of that evening confrontation with David. I listened and then tried again to reassure her that I would survive. I talked with her about my own hard-learned understanding of letting go, of relinquishing. I tried to explain the belief I now held that, for all of us on this earth, life is not permanent. It carries no guarantees of love, or fairness, or freedom from pain. It is its own journey and task.

On this day, Ellen put away her need to bring David and me together. She believed, as Frances did, that I would be all right. She went on, during her remaining time, to share in putting some pleasure or joy into each day.

And we had good times—we went to parks and beaches. We shared with friends—and we went alone. Sometimes we just drove, threading our way slowly along country roads. Sometimes as David or I drove, Ellen sat up and watched the passing landscape, catching and imprinting these sights on her mind. Sometimes she lay back, tired and sad, dreamily looking out into the lacy shadows of the trees flickering over us as we drove along. We found comfort and serenity in these drives. Some of those outings were small jewels of pure delight.

For Ellen, the need to hold on to life for our sake, to provide a link between us, had come to an end. She held on now for her own sake.

Novato, California
August 20, 1972

Dear Chris,

I haven't written for a very unthoughtful reason. I've been out hobbling around and doing quite well!—having very good times. Chris, I haven't felt so good since about directly after the surgery. The pain has just decreased immensely. I pray it keeps like this. I remember times earlier when I would wake up in the morning and think, "Oh God, got to face another day of pain." Those times seem such long past . . .

I'm running a fever of 100 to 103 degrees. My doctor believes it could very well be a protein breakdown. You see my kind of tumor is made out of protein, so if some of the cells are breaking down faster than the others are growing, I'm in luck. It means my abdominal tumor may be shrinking. On the other hand, if the protein cells break down at the same rate as the others grow, the tumor stays about the same size. It's surprising how much medical knowledge I've gained.

My mother is taking a two-week math course which she really digs. And of course she worries about me being totally alone all day. So for the first week Jan came over each morning from her house to stick around here. We had fantastic times. Yesterday, got back from a picnic in a very beautiful park—spreading shade trees over very green grass. Most important, out of all the times I spent with her, we could just be together comfortably. She is a very good and close friend.

El

11

In August, Ellen met Emily, a small girl fighting her own battle against leukemia.

I had become involved with a group of parents who had organized to help each other in the fight against childhood cancer. I went to many evening meetings, participating in adult planning and activities. Ellen regretted that there was no place for her at these meetings. She remained interested, frequently wanting to know about the children and their parents.

Our family had offered to spend some summer afternoons and evenings in the work of preparing cards for the year's fund-raising event. Emily's mother, sprightly and gay, seemingly always cheerful, brought the cards and envelopes to us, and brought Emily for a brief visit.

Like her mother, Emily seemed undaunted by her illness. She looked sturdy and healthy, with glowing cheeks and bright eyes. Though Ellen reached out to her, she held back, somewhat intimidated perhaps by Ellen's thin fragile appearance.

After Emily and her mother had left, as we worked on the cards and envelopes, Ellen asked about Emily. Did Emily know about her illness? Would she die? Could she be saved?

And out of my limited knowledge about Emily and her illness, I answered as best I could. Emily knew she had a serious illness. She knew that she needed treatment to fight the illness. I did not know if Emily would die. I knew that children did die of leukemia. I did not know if she could be saved. I did know that her parents and doctors were trying to save her.

Ellen listened and nodded.

12

Novato, Calif.
August 25, 1972

Barron,

You are someone who has come very close to me. There's no question of good or bad influences. You said yourself you were here for me and I like it that way. I think I have been here at times when you have needed me and maybe even sometimes when you haven't.

It never was important to me why you were in prison; it isn't now. I felt you would tell me when it felt right for you. I don't know if I pushed you into telling me, but I don't think I did.

When I read the first page of your letter, I felt a total sinking in me and confusion about what I could say to you—maybe some comforting words. But I think, like me, you've heard all those lines and words and it isn't what you need now or what you really want to hear. What I feel coming back to me again when I read your words, is my feeling of likeness to you. We are both prisoners. In their different ways our worlds limit us. I had said to you after my surgery, that I was no longer a captive because I'd been freed of pain. But in truth, the pain was not my prison; my illness is. I have in many ways accepted my situation—to some extent, just as you must have yours.

I have a lot of hope for you come October. Struggle on, because without struggle there is no life. This is something you have taught me.

I very much like being your adopted sister. May I hereby claim you as my brother?

You put a thought in my head when you talked about your poetry. People do write what they have learned, what their worlds have taught them. You need to express whatever your surrounding world is showing you. At this time it is some very ugly things that

*must come out in some way. I'm sending you the poems I wrote when
I was so knocked out by pain that I didn't know anything else,
except anger and feelings of—why me!*

*I wrote another poem I'm sending. It was very strange the way
it came about. A little girl named Emily came over with her
mother. We are helping in a cancer program, and they were
delivering some things.*

*Emily has leukemia. She knows how sick she is, yet she is so
alive and curious. She is one of the most loving and happy children
I've met. She radiates a glow toward people.*

*They stayed a while and we talked. Emily is in second grade,
she told me. She seemed shy of me, but very curious at the same time.*

*After they left, I picked up pencil and paper and the words
seemed to flow from my hand.*

*The cards you sent were really great. The first one cheered me
up much. Hey, who says you can't write poetry with feelings other
than angry ones? I liked your poem very much. Give my special
hellos and love to your comrades.*

> *Hey brother,*
> *I love you,*
> *El*

August, 1972

*Emily has a beautiful smile.
She laughs and she will sing for you.
Beautiful dream child
Watches the sun and sky.
Why is she one of them who must die.*

*Emily has bright eyes.
They leave their mark on you
By a sparkle that says, "Hello,
I'm kind of shy of you."*

Dear wild child Emily, why will
It be you who will go.

Ellen

13

August had been a month of well-being. Though she was thin and could eat little, Ellen was comfortable and relatively free from pain. Skilled prescription and management of medicines maintained a delicate balance of body functions.

September came. We returned to the high school, so that Ellen could register for courses and request home teachers. She met concern and commiseration with cheerfulness and outward optimism.

With misgiving, I arranged to begin my own teaching year. I knew that I would not be able to see the school year out, but I hoped to establish a good learning situation for my class and to teach as long as Ellen could function well without my daytime presence. I knew that, at some not too distant time, Ellen's present plateau would end and the downward path would resume. I knew too that when that time came, I would find a good substitute teacher and would return to my days at home with Ellen. We made plans for a young housekeeper to be with Ellen when Kathleen was not there. We planned the medical appointments again for after-school hours. All of this depended on Ellen's present feeling of well-being, her stated wish to have me return to school, the proximity of my school to our home, and the willing cooperativeness of the school administration.

So the school year began. The focus of the days shifted. Yet the emphasis remained the same. We were still living each day for itself. To us, *now* meant just one day at a time. And into *now* we continued to put what we could of pleasure and accomplishment.

As September passed, a rhythm was established. Kathleen and the young housekeeper shared the daytime responsibilities with me. David and I shared responsibility for Ellen's nighttime care. Anne and Jana visited often, providing pleasure and support. On weekends we enjoyed days of shared activities and outings.

This balance and rhythm ended in late September when it became clear that Ellen was weakening day by day. She was too tired to eat and too weak to move around. It became too difficult to continue her nightly bathroom duties, and she reluctantly acceded to Dr. Alton's recommendations: she allowed Anne to insert the bladder catheter, relieving her of this tyranny.

During that last week in September, it was clear that Ellen had begun to disentangle herself from this life. We arranged to take leave from our jobs; first David, then I.

IX

1972: OCTOBER
Departure

I was not aware of the moment when I first crossed the threshhold of this life.
What was the power that made me open out into this vast mystery like a bud in the forest at midnight!
When in the morning I looked upon the light I felt in a moment that I was no stranger in this world, that the inscrutable without name and form had taken me in its arms in the form of my mother.
Even so, in death the same unknown will appear as ever known to me. And because I love this life, I know I shall love death as well . . . . .

Rabindranath Tagore, *Gitanjali*, 95

1

The sun scorched through early October haze. It was Sunday, mid-afternoon. David worked outside. He tore weeds from the ivy, commanding the tender plants to grow, to survive, to outwit the ever-munching deer.

He greeted Dr. Alton; then Adele, a neighbor who had followed close behind. He remained outside with her, talking of plants, and deer, and houses, and weather—neighbor talk—while the doctor entered the house.

Dr. Alton came in, light-stepped for a large man, sad and gentle, carrying in his hand a fragile-stemmed yellow rose of peace. He had phoned earlier, offering to visit, dreading the task of explaining his coming absence.

Sunk in her large black chair, Ellen lay half-dreaming, musing, head turned toward the windows and the haze of blue sky above California sun-burned tree tops. Her body, now a framework of bones covered with skin, could have been the shell of an aged woman. With eyes half-closed, her face was gaunt, the skin of her cheeks and chin drawn tight over protruding bones.

With a sad smile and an almost gallant gesture, he held out the rose. Her eyes opened, the depths of brown smiled back at him. I watched, and saw the outraged body. But I saw, too, what was within. The terribly thin, consumed, soon to be discarded body was at odds with Ellen's eyes. Her eyes were still beautiful, or perhaps more beautiful than ever: deep brown, sad yet serene.

His medical bag set down, the doctor sat with Ellen, and we talked. For me it was a sharing of infinitely precious time. What was it for Jana who sat, legs drawn up, listening, not speaking, surely knowing that the long vigil was soon to end? What was it for David who had remained outside with Adele, and the ivy and weeds, to safeguard the precious moment inside the house?

Quiet, soft words were spoken, words of groping for meaning, of fear and dread, yet words of strength. The doctor asked about pain, his mission to provide comfort. He and Ellen talked of the many medicines—facilitators of body functions which had controlled her hours. She complained with a bitterness, not sharp or acid but somehow detached, yet wondering still how this could be happening to her.

"I can't take so many pills. I can't get them down." The facts of her life closing down, of body functions becoming too difficult to carry out—these facts were being stated without anguish.

"I don't feel like eating. My dad wants me to eat."

The doctor quietly supported her withdrawal. I echoed his words.

"Eat what you can."

"Eat what you like."

"Take the most important pills first. You can let the others wait until you feel like taking them."

Which were the important pills? Not many now. Days earlier the long-dreaded catheter had been inserted to facilitate the failing bladder's work. She no longer needed medicine to moderate that painful spasm. Bowel function was something I now aided, having been shown by Anne and Dr. Alton how this could be done.

Our talk shifted away from the concrete problems of relieving pain and easing discomfort, of reassuring Ellen that she could eat what she wished and take pills when she felt them necessary.

We talked then of living and dying. We knew that Ellen had begun the process of separating herself from the body which had so impeded her. She spoke of her sorrow that she would miss many experiences she once wanted and took for granted would be her due. She was afraid—but somehow sadly and serenely so, not with apprehension. She was sad that life was ending.

We shared speculations and personal beliefs about the

survival of the human spirit, about immortality and what that might be. Ellen stated hers simply. She hoped that she would contribute to the replenishment of the earth's vital resources. She hoped for a place in nature's eternal cycle of growth and decay and growth. She did not seem to seek or ask for assurance of a more personal immortality.

The doctor then explained that he was leaving on a short trip to give a lecture in Southern California. He would return in a few days. He would telephone her in the meantime.

Ellen's response was tranquil, unalarmed. Later, as she lay drowsing, reflecting, Dr. Alton shared with me a brief moment of speculation and prediction. He was concerned about his coming brief absence. He felt that Ellen's death was near. My response came from my feelings about the relationship that had grown and matured between them.

"Don't worry about being gone. She'll wait for you."

He gave practical explicit information: another doctor was available, who would come at any time if called. And, again he reassured me, he would telephone from Southern California.

2

Monday came and passed into evening. It had been a beautiful day—an early rain, light and almost golden, had fallen on the burned hills. Ellen rested, moved from chair to sofa and back again by David who now lifted and carried her, light and frail, encumbered by catheter and bag. She had put aside self-consciousness about the equipment—it was a day when she seemed able to ignore the downward pull of her body's limitations. She ate lightly, disinterested in food, but willing to sustain her body with whatever nourishment she could get down.

As the day passed, she shared it with people she loved. Norah had come. Jana and Kathleen stayed nearby. We played records; we talked; we enjoyed watching the outside rain as it cleared and cooled the hot dry California autumn. Rick and I baked cookies. David, ever-available to Ellen's call, worked on papers he had brought from his office. The outward forms and actions were commonplace. The tone was of peace and tranquility, of hiatus and respite from pain and emergency.

One by one the friends left as the afternoon ended.

3

The evening meal was behind us. Ellen lay back in her chair, while David and Jana sat nearby. In the unscreened fireplace, a fire burned. It was cheerful, comforting and warm.

More visitors arrived: Judy's mother, not with Judy, but with another girl, a friend of Judy's older brother. The talk was quiet, purposefully light, and out of it came a request from the visiting girl to play Ellen's flute. It was well-intentioned, a wish to share a moment of pleasure.

She played and for Ellen it became a moment of stark recognition and acknowledgement. She sat upright.

"I'm going to play my flute now."

Protests and explanations.

"Not now."

"You're tired."

Indignation flared in Ellen's eyes. Her cheeks, pale and cold, now flushed with her effort.

"Then I'm going to sit in the blue chair!"

The blue chair. Across the room. David moved in quickly, lovingly. He gathered her in his arms and placed her carefully on the blue chair. I hurried to kneel nearby. A vague, nameless dread stirred within me—that this, right now, was a moment of crisis.

"See, I can sit here like anyone else. I can cross my legs!" Outrage and assertion in Ellen's voice. The assertion of *I will*. And then she crumbled.

"I'm so tired."

The visitors moved to the door. "It's late. We'll go now."

"Thank you for coming."

With polite exchanges they left, as David carried Ellen to her bedroom. There he sat with her. Ellen, exhausted, put her head on his shoulder; his arm encircled her as they rested on the edge of the bed.

Within me, the forboding began to take shape and definition. I spoke words of my love. "Oh Ellen, I know it feels so good to have his arm around you."

Ellen's eyes told of being only partly present. Yet she had heard, and her eyes said she too knew the love.

"I think I'd better lie down. I'm tired."

Again the dread, no longer nameless, strong and insistent now, inside of me. Tender, gentle movements from David as he helped Ellen to lie down. No more words. Our eyes locked—Ellen's and mine—and we looked deep into each other's beings. Each of us knew that the time had come. This was the moment.

Silence . . . as Ellen's eyes opened very wide. Those brown eyes, so deep and warm, disengaged from my inquiring gaze, and she was gone. Ellen was gone. The wracked and weary body lay, an empty shell, at rest on the bed that had been Ellen's.

Epilogue

We buried Ellen on a quiet hillside, shaded by tall branching oaks and stately cypress. It rained intermittently—soft, light rain. The rain stopped briefly as we said our last goodbyes, each of us alone again in our own personal and unique blendings of sorrow and relief.

A winter of numbness and blind groping movement through days and nights followed. Then we went our own ways, each to put together into some usable fabric the threads of our memories of Ellen and her last two years.

Jana returned to Berkeley—to work there in a clinic. Her memories are her very own. She took Ellen's flute with her. When we come together, now two separate adults, she sometimes plays the flute and we share feelings and words about those days.

David is building his own life, focusing again on his career. We are able to come together now with respect, friendship, and pleasure. Surely he carries with him his knowledge of the love and devotion with which he saw Ellen through.

And I continue on this fantastic journey of day following day, clear in my own mind now that people belong to life, not to each other. For me, each day is a treasure which yields back only what I put into it. It was of overwhelming importance to me to put into the days which followed Ellen's death, this recording—fragmentary though it is—of our days of loving.